Khalid Hamid was born in 1991 in Srinagar, Kashmir, and attended the Tyndale Biscoe School. He later earned a Master's degree in Human Resources and moved to the United Arab Emirates after his studies. In the UAE, Khalid pursued a career in human resources, where he had the privilege of interacting with people from all walks of life. In his free time outside his 9-to-5 job, Khalid discovered his creative side. He enjoyed painting, poetry, doing voice acting, and writing for fun. Khalid Hamid's life is a blend of work and art, always seeking new ways to express his creativity.

To My beautiful Wife Irma and my wonderful daughter Imara, you both have made me a better man.

# Khalid Hamid Kashtwari

## KASTOOR

Austin Macauley Publishers™
LONDON · CAMBRIDGE · NEW YORK · SHARJAH

**Copyright © Khalid Hamid Kashtwari 2024**

The right of Khalid Hamid Kashtwari to be identified as author of this work has been asserted by the author in accordance with Federal Law No. (7) of UAE, Year 2002, Concerning Copyrights and Neighboring Rights.

All rights reserved. No part of this publication may be reproduced, stored in a retrieval system, or transmitted in any form or by any means, electronic, mechanical, photocopying, recording, or otherwise, without the prior permission of the publishers.

Any person who commits any unauthorized act in relation to this publication may be liable to legal prosecution and civil claims for damages.

The story, experiences, and words are the author's alone.

The age group that matches the content of the books has been classified according to the age classification system issued by the Ministry of Culture and Youth.

ISBN – 9789948756057 – (Paperback)
ISBN – 9789948756064 – (E-Book)

Application Number: MC-10-01-3125484
Age Classification: 13+

Printer Name: iPrint Global Ltd
Printer Address: Witchford, England

First Published 2024
AUSTIN MACAULEY PUBLISHERS FZE
Sharjah Publishing City
P.O Box [519201]
Sharjah, UAE
www.austinmacauley.ae
+971 655 95 202

This story would not have been possible without the contributions, ideas, and collaboration of many people who dedicated their time and creativity to shape this narrative. I extend my heartfelt thanks to my brother Nadeem, my best friends Jibran and Abrar for giving me opinions on my crazy ideas and to all those who made this journey possible. This project had its origins in a dream shared by myself and my friends, Abrar, Burhan, Waleed, and others. What began as a script for a movie, born out of youthful enthusiasm, was brought to life as a written narrative when life's responsibilities and changing careers redirected our paths. It stands as a tribute to the dreams we once held and as a testament to the enduring power of friendship and collaboration. Finally, my deepest thanks to the talented and dedicated writers, editors, and creators who bring stories to life and share their expertise with the world. You are the lifeblood of the literary world, and I salute your craft.

# Table of Contents

| | |
|---|---|
| Chapter 1: Family | 12 |
| Chapter 2: The village Boy | 23 |
| Chapter 3: The Lost Parental Love | 38 |
| Chapter 4: The Wedding | 48 |
| Chapter 5: The Fall | 56 |
| Chapter 6: Rebirth | 68 |
| Chapter 7: Worst News | 79 |
| Chapter 8: Pursuit of Truth | 95 |
| Chapter 9: The Lawman | 109 |
| Chapter 10: The Investigation | 118 |
| Chapter 11: The Fracture | 125 |
| Chapter 12: The Prey | 142 |
| Chapter 13: Unshaken | 151 |
| Chapter 14: The Game | 160 |
| Chapter 15: Save the Soul | 180 |

Epigraph:
"Truth is rarely pure and never simple." Oscar Wilde

# Chapter 1
# Family

Nestled between the great Himalayan mountains, where the land reaches up to touch the sky, lies the beautiful valley of Kashmir. Like a precious jewel held gently in nature's hands, this enchanting place captures the gaze of the world with its charm. A land where heaven and earth dance together in harmony with green meadows meeting blue skies and the air echoing legends and longing.

The shining waters of Dal Lake reflect the stately chinar trees, snowy peaks and the dreams of generations who call this valley home. The winding alleys of Srinagar with wooden houses and carved balconies stand guard over a time gone by. Here, time ambles slowly, listening to tales whispered by winds that have journeyed through the ages.

As the sun rises over Dal Lake's tranquil expanse, its shimmering water seems to promise a new beginning. The call to prayer echoes through the air, a melody reminding all of the faith that has anchored generations in this land.

In the heart of Srinagar, where time has etched its mark into the very stones paving the streets, a crowd of young souls gathers at Islamia College of Science and Commerce. This college with its emerald green lawns encircling red-brick buildings, that wear the patina of history, has imparted education for over 80 years. The faces of these new students show hope, uncertainty and a touch of youthful excitement. This scene has occurred countless times, yet for each person, this moment is unique. The students stand in this vibrant tapestry of youth. The college admission rituals, a dance of paperwork and waiting form a bridge between their past and the possibilities ahead.

Each student is carrying bunch of papers in his hand, these papers signifying stories of dreams nurtured despite hardship, of family sacrifices through their own storms and quiet resolve to rise above circumstances that would define their future. As the line inches forward, lively conversations buzz like bees around a blooming garden. Hopes and dreams are exchanged, creating shared energy that fills the very air they breathe.

It is the busiest time of year on campus with students filling out applications, choosing academic paths. Some are pursuing science, others business or commerce degrees. Shahid, Abrar and Burhan had already made their choices and they unanimously chose business studies, although what mattered most was staying together. These best friends had been inseparable since childhood, despite different social classes.

Abrar came from a lower-middle-class family and possessed boyish looks that belied the depth of his insight. His ever-present smile was like a beacon inviting others into his world of excitement and spontaneity. Despite his youthful appearance, Abrar's heart held an old soul, rich with wisdom and an innate ability to find joy in the simplest of moments.

Like thousands of other Kashmiris, his father went missing during the militancy era in Kashmir, known as "Tehreeq" right after the army detained him. Now, his mother relied on the pension of her deceased husband and earned extra money by making curtains, shawls and blankets at home. She still carried old pictures of her missing husband to rallies where wives and children of the missing men gather, urging the government to search for them. Like many other families, she believed he was still alive and will return to them one day.

Abrar was a devoted son who would help his mother in household chores and even with the embroidery of curtains and shawls. Despite their economic hardship, Fathima, Abrar's mother, wanted him to study at the best schools in the valley. She had to sell all her gold jewelry received from her family when she got married – one by one, to afford a good education for Abrar. Lately, times had been tough and they had started to even rent out the first floor of their house to make ends meet.

Shahid came from an upper-middle-class family. Standing tall and broad-shouldered, he exuded a quiet confidence that drew people towards him. His presence was magnetic, a blend of strength and warmth that made him approachable to all. With his expressive eyes and neatly trimmed beard, he commanded respect without demanding it. His father worked as a health officer in the local municipality and his mother was a homemaker. He had two sisters and a younger brother. Being the eldest, Shahid looked up to his parents and plans to start a business in Kashmir to create job opportunities and bring much-needed economic changes to the valley.

Burhan possessed a captivating blend of qualities that made him stand out. His face seemed to strike a unique balance between femininity and a mature sophistication, sculpted with a precise artistry that both caught the eye and stirred an air of intrigue. But Burhan's appeal went beyond his looks; it was rooted in his deep understanding of the world around him. His thoughtful nature and compassionate demeanor naturally drew people to him, making him a trusted confidant and an unwavering source of support.

While his family could be described as upper middle class, verging on wealth, Burhan currently resided in the home of his maternal uncle. His journey began in Dubai, where he was born and attended kindergarten and schooling. However, his life took a significant turn at the age of 7 when his parents separated. In the midst of a custody battle, his parents made an unusual decision: they left him in the care of his grandmother. It seemed neither of them wanted to gain sole custody, choosing instead to let him continue his education in Kashmir. The understanding was that, upon graduation, he would have the autonomy to decide whether to stay with his father or mother.

Burhan held a deep affection for his grandmother, cherishing the time he spent with her. However, life challenges struck again when, at the age of 15, his beloved grandmother passed away. Once more he found himself in a state of flux, this time compelled to reside with his uncle and aunt. The ongoing conflicts between the couple meant that Burhan struggled to receive the attention and love he so deeply desired from his parents. His aunt and uncle, whom he had been living with for the past five years, could not entirely fill the void left by his parents. In this time of need, Burhan found solace in two dear best friends who provided him with love and companionship, making them his most cherished companions.

The friendship of Burhan, Shahid and Abrar was forged 12 years ago in the hallways of their school. They were eight years old and together converged to create a bond that went beyond the ordinary. From their first encounter it was clear that their connection was something special. Brought together by a combination of chance and shared interests, their friendship had stood the test of time. While other students hustled and bustled through the corridors, these three found solace in each other's company.

Unlike many of their peers, who thrived on sports and extracurricular activities, Abrar, Burhan and Shahid found their own kind of magic in each other's presence. While the soccer field, cricket pitches and basketball courts echoed with the sounds of competitive fervor, these friends found joy in the quieter moments, in conversations that meandered through myriad topics and in laughter that echoed through empty classrooms. They shared a collective aversion to conformity, rejecting the notion that fun could only be found within the confines of organized sports. Instead, they found delight in inventing their own games, creating imaginary worlds where they were explorers, charting uncharted territories or detectives solving baffling mysteries. Their shared imaginations knew no bounds and they reveled in every moment they spent together.

It was in these moments, away from the spotlight of traditional activities that their bond truly flourished. Their friendship was the canvas upon which they painted their dreams, their aspirations, and their individualities. Each brought a distinct color to the masterpiece they were creating, turning their friendship into a mosaic of laughter, shared secrets and unspoken support. As the years passed, their connection deepened. Their camaraderie was a refuge, a sanctuary where they could be themselves without reservation. They celebrated each other's victories and weathered the storms of life as a united front. Their preferences may have set them apart from the mainstream, but it was this very uniqueness that bound them together in a way that was unbreakable. In a world that often tried to define them by the norms it prescribed, Abrar, Burhan, and Shahid found their own definition of friendship.

As they grew up, their friendship had become even stronger and today was the beginning of a new chapter in the lives. These three young boys stood nervously at the imposing gates of the institution. This was no ordinary college; it carried a sense of unease and uncertainty. Most Kashmiri colleges had a reputation that preceded them. Intimidating gangs prowled the corridors, looking for trouble and asserting their dominance. The air around the corners of the campus was often thick with the pungent scent of cigarettes and occasionally marijuana, as stoners roamed freely, their minds perpetually clouded. And then there were the criminals, those who had once tasted the bitterness of prison life but now sought redemption through education.

All the other students could feel the friendship of Abrar, Burhan, and Shahid, some were a little jealous, and some made fun of them comparing their comradery to "gay" behavior. Although their presence alone seemed to radiate a different kind of energy—one that demanded respect and yet caused trepidation. It was not that the boys themselves were troublemakers; rather, they possessed an unyielding bond and an unwavering belief in their camaraderie. They unconsciously believed that if they were together, they could face anything the world threw their way.

However, there was one aspect of their college experience that they hadn't anticipated—sharing classes with girls. Having attended all-boys schools since their kindergarten days, the presence of the fairer sex was an unfamiliar territory for them. As they walked into their first class, their eyes involuntarily wandered to the other side of the room, where a group of girls sat, their mere presence captivating. Their professor, an observant individual with a discerning gaze, was quick to notice the boys' distraction. Clearing his throat, he called out, 'Gentlemen, the board is where your attention should be focused, not on your female classmates. You can do that outside of my class.'

Blushing with embarrassment, the boys swiftly averted their gazes and tried to regain their composure. They had never been caught in such a compromising situation before. However, despite their best efforts, their curiosity proved difficult to suppress. Their eyes would inevitably wander back to the girls, only to be met with a gentle but firm reminder from the professor.

After a few days, and the trio slowly acclimated to their newfound co-ed environment. The girls, for their part, were accustomed to this dynamic and continued with their studies undeterred by the boys' wandering eyes. Gradually, the boys began to understand the importance of discipline and respect in this new setting. Conversations sparked, bonds formed, and the girls became more than just objects of curiosity. They were individuals with their own dreams, aspirations, and stories to tell. The boys found themselves eager to engage with their female classmates on an intellectual level, cherishing the opportunity to gain experience from their unique perspectives.

One sunny afternoon, after their classes had come to an end, the three boys embarked on an exploratory mission around the sprawling campus. They wandered through the corridors, traversed the gardens, and followed winding paths, curious to uncover any hidden gems that lay concealed within the college's boundaries. Their wanderings eventually led them to a secluded corner of the campus, where they stumbled upon a forgotten treasure—an unfinished building structure engulfed by a thick cluster of lush trees. Intrigued, they approached the structure, and discovered a narrow staircase leading to the rooftop. Climbing up the stairs with a mixture of excitement and anticipation, they emerged onto the roof and were greeted by a breathtaking view. From this vantage point, they could see the entire campus, stretching out before them like a tapestry woven with dreams and possibilities. They started visiting this spot every day during lunch and after their classes to escape the pressures of their studies. The world seemed distant and insignificant from this hidden perch, allowing them to temporarily escape the pressures of their academic lives.

One day, as they settled down in their secret spot, feeling hidden from prying eyes, Burhan, always one to infuse meaning into the simplest of things, suggested they give this newfound haven a name. The boys pondered, their minds adrift in a sea of imagination until Burhan spoke up, his voice carrying a touch of nostalgia.

'Let's call it Kastoor Penj,' he suggested, his eyes shining with fervor. When his friends turned to him inquisitively, he began to explain, his words taking on a melodic quality. 'Kastoor, my friends, is a flycatcher—a bird that used to migrate to Kashmir from Africa every spring for thousands of years. But something has changed. Recently, they have stopped coming, and no one knows why. It's a loss, a break in the natural rhythm. Kastoor Penj will be our way of honoring that loss, reminding us of the fragile beauty of the world around us.'

Abrar's eyes lit up with curiosity as he looked at Burhan. 'Kastoor Penj sounds kind of depressing,' he remarked with a smile.

'Can't we think of a more upbeat name for our secret hangout?' Shahid glanced over at Burhan, noticing the glint of excitement in his friend's eyes despite his solemn words.

'You know, I kind of, like this name,' Shahid said lightly.

'Isn't there a place already with this name though?'

Burhan's momentary nostalgia lifted as he looked at his friends, a grin spreading across his face. 'Yes, there is a place near Maqdoom sahab's shrine with the same name,' he replied.

'Kastoor Penj can be our name for now but for now, let's just keep this spot our secret. I doubt many other students will find their way here anyway.' The three friends exchanged smiles, already feeling a sense of ownership over this newfound refuge.

Burhan suddenly exclaimed, 'Guys, have you noticed that some of the girls here have been checking us out lately? I think it might be a good idea for us to step up our style game and make a lasting impression.'

Shahid nods in agreement, his eyes lighting up with excitement, 'You're spot on, Burhan. Just today, I couldn't help but notice this stunning girl from our economics class flashing me a friendly smile!'

Burhan grins, fully acknowledging Shahid's enthusiasm. 'That's all great, but trust me, we all need to upgrade our wardrobes. This isn't high school anymore. Let's go to the city for some clothes shopping tomorrow, what do you say?'

Abrar hesitates, a hint of concern crossing his face, 'That sounds like a lot of fun, guys, but I'm not sure I can afford it. My mom has already spent so much on my admission and books this semester.'

Burhan is quick to reassure him, showing his considerate side in a funny voice trying his best not to sound condescending, 'Don't worry about it, my friend! I've got your back. I'll cover the expenses for your new clothes as a gift.'

Abrar hesitates, touched by Burhan's generosity. 'Oh, you really don't have to do that, Burhan. You know I'm not used to people buying me gifts.'

Burhan insists with a warm smile. 'Come on, Abrar, I insist! It's my treat. We will all look sharp. You cannot say no to that.'

Abrar finally relents, appreciative of the gesture, 'Well...all right, if you're sure. Thanks a lot, Burhan. I really appreciate it.'

The following day, the trio rendezvous in the bustling city for their shopping adventure.

Burhan takes the lead with enthusiasm, 'All right, guys, let's make this shopping trip count! I'm thinking jeans, stylish jackets, and some cool T-shirts.'

Shahid chimes in with excitement, 'Sounds like a plan! I could definitely use some fresh sneakers too.'

Abrar gazes at the array of options, his eyes widening with wonder, 'Wow, look at all these choices. I've never shopped for clothes like this before. Thanks again for doing this, Burhan.'

Burhan reassures him with a warm smile, 'Don't mention it! Just pick out what makes you feel confident. Todays on me.'

Abrar, a bit bashful but grateful, remembers that Burhan is like family to him. With a grateful smile, he responds, 'In that case, I better not hold back!' Abrar's eye meets a black leather jacker, he shouts in awe, 'This leather jacket looks amazing.'

Burhan encourages him with a nod, 'Go for it, clothes are meant to be worn, not just admired. It's yours, my friend.'

Abrar beams with gratitude, 'You're the best, Burhan.'

In that heartwarming moment of friendship, Burhan's unwavering support shone bright. His incredible generosity and ability to uplift his friends truly made him exceptional.

# Chapter 2
# The Village Boy

The quaint town of Patan is a hidden gem tucked away in the mountains of Kashmir. Narrow cobblestone streets wind through old wooden houses with intricately carved windows and sloping rustic roofs. In the distance, snow-capped peaks pierce the horizon, framing the valley with their rugged magnificence. The sound of gurgling streams combines with the faint echoes of call to prayers touched by the wind.

In the village square there was an old tailoring shop, this shop has been operating since last 40 years by Ghulam Mohammed. His only son, Waleed, whom he loved the most in this world, had an unpretentious charm that emanated from his patchy beard and fair skin. His appearance might have been ordinary, but his presence was anything but. With eyes that held a quiet curiosity and a smile that radiated warmth, he brought a sense of calm to their boisterous adventures.

Despite his lack of formal education, Ghulam Mohammed had a deep desire for Waleed to receive a good education. Waleed possessed exceptional abilities, easily memorizing information, and a deep desire for learning mathematics.

Waleed was an only child and cherished the time he spent with his father. After school, he would sit at his father's shop, still dressed in his school uniform, and complete his homework. The tailoring shop was a treasure trove of fabrics, colors, and dreams spun into reality. Nestled within a bustling street, the shop was a haven where bolts of cloth were transformed into intricate designs under the skillful hands of the master. Upon entering, one was greeted by the harmonious hum of sewing machines, the rhythmic cadence of creativity that brought life to the inanimate. Waleed's mother would often send Waleed to his father's shop with a kettle of salt "sheer" tea, which the duo would always share with customers who visited them. The air carried the scent of freshly cut fabric, a scent that held within it the promise of new beginnings and stylish transformations. After school as Waleed would join and help his father with tailoring work, he would amaze his father with what he had learned that day, sharing fascinating facts such as how stars are formed and how the sun is also a star, around which the Earth revolves. His father would playfully argue with Waleed, teasingly questioning the concept of the Earth revolving around the much smaller sun. Waleed would passionately explain his theories, and his father took great pride in their intellectual conversations, often involving friends and locals in their discussions.

Their world felt small and beautiful as father and son shared these moments. However, life is unpredictable, and one day while Waleed was out running errands, his father collapsed from a heart attack. He was rushed to the local government hospital, where he lay on an old hospital bed. The hospital room enveloped Waleed in an atmosphere of muted light and barely audible whispers. The walls, painted in the gentlest hues of pale blue, silently witnessed the prevailing sense of disarray and despair. The air hung heavy with the clinical odor of antiseptics, a constant reminder of the medical realm that governed this place. Yet, it was abundantly clear that the hospital staff, including the doctors, fell short of the compassionate care patients deserved.

Hours seemed to stretch as they awaited any semblance of attention for Waleed's father. The medical team's apathy was palpable, their indifference more pronounced with every passing minute. The medication, desperately needed to alleviate his father's suffering was withheld, allowing his condition to deteriorate further. It was a disheartening testament to the callousness that pervaded the very heart of this healthcare institution.

Waleed, sitting beside his father, wondered if he was somehow to blame. His father, sensing his last breath approaching, beckoned Waleed closer and whispered his final words. 'You are my treasure. Never settle for less in life. Please go to college and make something of yourself. You are smarter than you know.' With tears streaming down his face, Waleed held his father tightly, unable to believe that this vibrant presence was now gone.

Waleed's mother was a simple, religious Muslim woman who found solace in prayer and hard work. After her husband's sudden death, she relied on her faith and the rhythms of the small apple orchard they owned to provide structure to her days. Each morning as the first rays of golden sunlight crept over the mountains, she would rise, perform her ablutions, and lose herself in the poetic verses of morning prayer. This daily devotion gave her strength and helped dull the ache of loss.

Her days were spent tending to the apple trees that had been her husband's pride and joy. She pruned and watered them with a diligence born of love, imagining that a part of her beloved still lived on through the fruits of his labor. In the cool of the evening, the melody of the azaan would draw her once more into prayerful reflection. Kneeling on her worn prayer mat, tasbih beads in hand, she whispered her hopes and worries to the Almighty.

Waleed was consumed with grief but also determined to honor his dying wish to pursue an education. However, the family's dire financial situation necessitated that Waleed start working immediately to support himself and his mother. With a heavy heart, he took his place behind the counter at his father's beloved tailoring shop. As he looked around at the shelves of fabric and the machines that had crafted countless dreams, memories of happy afternoons spent here flooded over him. He could almost see his father cutting cloth with skilled hands, hear his deep laughter ringing out.

Waleed slowly learned the tricks of the trade—how to take measurements, cut patterns, and stitch garments. His fingers fumbled with the sewing machine at first but gradually grew more confident. While he found some joy in creating beautiful apparel, his true passion was learning. At night, after the shop closed, he would pore over his old textbooks, transported back to those lively discussions with his father.

Weeks passed, and Waleed had a vivid dream one night. In his dream, his father appeared, questioning why he was defying his last wish. Waleed woke up, drenched in sweat and shaken. The next morning, he made a life-altering decision. He collected whatever savings he had and boarded a bus to Srinagar, the capital city of Kashmir. Looking out the bus window, he couldn't help but shed a tear, feeling both fear and determination in the face of the unknown.

As the bus reached the city, Waleed, having fallen asleep during the journey, woke up to find it parked at the station. He washed his face at an open tap, taking in the bustling noises and unfamiliar smells of the city. His first instinct was to call his neighbors, so that they could inform his mother, that he had left for the city to pursue his college admissions and that he would figure out a way to support himself and his mother.

Stepping onto the sprawling college grounds, Waleed's senses were overwhelmed by the buzzing activity around him. The admission process loomed ahead, a complex labyrinth of forms, questions, and document submissions that seemed to stretch infinitely. A sense of bewilderment washed over him as he fumbled with the admission officer's inquiries and struggled to produce the necessary papers. In this sea of uncertainty, he noticed a huddle of boys nearby, engrossed in conversation. Gathering his courage, he approached them with a mixture of hope and hesitation, seeking their assistance in this unfamiliar terrain.

This spontaneous encounter marked the introduction to Abrar, Shahid, and Burhan. Their faces radiated warmth as they patiently guided him through the bewildering maze of admissions. With reassuring smiles, they clarified his doubts, provided insights into the intricate process, and ensured that Waleed's submission was complete and accurate. Feeling an immense sense of gratitude, he thanked them for their invaluable help and set forth to navigate the remainder of his college admissions. Admission officer informed Waleed that the classes had started already weeks ago but luckily there was still one seat left. Waleed smiled as his admission was completed and they handed him his admission card.

After the formalities were settled, Waleed's path diverged into the city's streets, his quest now focused on securing a part-time job. The sewing skills he had inherited from his father were his most treasured possession, and he hoped to find employment at one of the tailoring shops that lined the bustling avenues. Yet, at every establishment he approached, he encountered closed doors and curt dismissals. As his spirits began to wane under the weight of rejection, Waleed's determination flickered like a dim flame, refusing to be extinguished.

Persistently, he continued his search, his weariness and hunger intensifying with each futile attempt. Finally, as if guided by fate, Waleed rested on a park bench and as he was getting ready to start again, he was astounded to find Burhan, the very person who had offered him a lifeline during his college admission predicament. A mixture of surprise and curiosity flooded Burhan's eyes as he questioned Waleed about his unexpected presence.

Waleed's cheeks flushed with embarrassment as he explained, 'I'm searching for a part-time job to support myself. My family is back in the village, I can do tailoring I learned it from my late father.' The admission of his family's circumstances and his father's recent passing hung in the air, revealing a vulnerability he hadn't intended to share.

Burhan's expression softened, and he deliberated for a moment before sharing a plan. Guiding Waleed to an impeccably presented men's tailoring establishment, Burhan engaged in a discreet conversation with the shop's owner. While Waleed waited with bated breath, he couldn't decipher the exchange between Burhan and the owner. Soon, Burhan returned, a smile tugging at the corners of his lips. 'I know him through my father. He's a good man. Let's see if he can help,' he reassured Waleed.

The owner approached Waleed, inquiring about his tailoring expertise. With newfound confidence, Waleed eloquently recounted his experiences collaborating with his father in the quaint village of Patan. The owner, testing Waleed's skills, assigned him a task that he completed with a mixture of apprehension and focus. Impressed by Waleed's precision and dedication, the owner extended an offer. He not only granted him the part-time job but also revealed that living quarters were available on the upper floors of the shop. Waleed's heart swelled with gratitude as he absorbed the terms and conditions. The owner assured him of a monthly salary of 4000 rupees, a figure that felt like a lifeline to Waleed's aspirations.

As they came out of the store, Burhan handed Waleed some money, confusion mingled with gratitude as he looked up at Burhan. 'What's this for?' he asked, genuinely surprised. Burhan's eyes twinkled with kindness.

'Consider it a little something to help you settle in,' he replied.

'You're just starting out, and I know how things can be. Use it for food, supplies, whatever you need.'

Waleed was moved by the gesture. He hadn't expected this, but it was a testament to the genuine care that existed in this kind young man. 'Thank you, but I will consider a loan and I will pay it back once I get my salary,' he said, his voice tinged with emotion.

'I appreciate it more than you know.'

Burhan chuckled softly. 'OK, OK, it's a loan but no need to thank me. We're college mates, and I can understand, it's not easy being in a new place.' Burhan left and with his spirits lifted, Waleed immediately went to a nearby phone booth shop, called his neighbor, requesting them to inform his mother about the good news. His neighbor shouted from the window and Waleed's mother ran to their home to talk to her son. Through tears of joy, he gave her the news, apologized to leave in such a way and reassured his mother that he would send her half of his salary every month and continue his studies diligently. His mother, filled with happiness and pride, simply told him to take care of himself and expressed her gratitude for such positive news.

As he went into the college to attend his first class with his old, rugged bag, filled to brim with most of his belongings, he walked with a certain awkwardness, his clothes seemed a bit too casual for the college environment, and his village accent stood out amongst the city-slicker tones. His arrival was anything but inconspicuous, and a few curious glances were exchanged between students. But his mission was clear to him, he had to graduate top in his class and make his late father proud. With this sense of purpose, Waleed embarked on a new chapter in his life, driven by the memory of his father's last words and the determination to create a better future for himself and his mother. Waleed immersed himself in his studies, attending classes with an insatiable thirst for knowledge. He found solace in the familiar rhythm of academic pursuits, diving into books, engaging in stimulating discussions, and pushing the boundaries of his intellect.

The following week in college, Shahid, Abrar, and Burhan found themselves seated in the classroom, their attention divided between the lecture and the occasional glance towards Samreen, a captivating presence in their midst. Shahid struggled to tear his eyes away from her, finding himself entranced by her every movement. And to his surprise, Samreen noticed his stolen glances, reciprocating with a smile whenever their eyes met. Shahid's heart skipped a beat, and he could not help but return her smile, though his bashfulness was evident.

As the class finally ended, the boys made their way to the bustling hallway, eager to escape the confines of the classroom. But their plans for a peaceful break were abruptly interrupted by a commotion echoing through the corridor. Shouts filled the air, drawing their attention towards a chaotic scene that unfolded before them—a full-blown fight between Rahil Khan, a formidable senior, and a new student who had recently joined their college.

Rahil, a towering figure at 6'2" with the build of a tank, unleashed his fury upon the junior, mercilessly attacking him. Shahid's curiosity got the better of him, and he couldn't resist asking a fellow student about the new student's identity. With a hint of awe in his voice, the student responded, 'I think his name is Waleed. He's from some village up in the mountains. Rahil was just messing with him, but Waleed stood up to him and landed a punch right on Rahil's face. Insane, right?'

'Rahil's gonna make him regret it.'

Burhan, ever the peacemaker, stepped forward, attempting to intervene and stop the escalating violence. He had recognized Waleed and knew he had to help him. However, his efforts were in vain as Rahil shrugged him off and continued to rain blows upon Waleed's defenseless form. Unable to stand idly by Shahid and Abrar sprang into action, charging towards the brawl, determined to free Waleed from Rahil's clutches.

Rahil, burning with anger, redirected his fury toward the two newcomers. He yelled, 'Who gave you the right to interfere? This is between him and me! Go away!' However, Shahid, undaunted, attempted to reason with him, saying,

'Come on, Rahil, let it go. He's just a younger student.' Enraged, Rahil forcefully pushed Shahid aside. Shahid, aware of his strength advantage, prepared to confront Rahil, but just as the tension peaked, Burhan suddenly unleashed a powerful punch that landed squarely on Rahil's eye. In an instant, Rahil collapsed to the ground, knocked out cold.

Just as the boys caught their breath, their triumph was interrupted by the arrival of the professor, his voice laced with fury, 'What the hell is going on here?' Panic surged through the group, and they scattered in all directions, including Waleed, who quickly joined them in their mad dash for safety. They sought refuge in their secret hideout, a place known only to them, lovingly dubbed "kastoor penj".

Within the safety of their hideout, the boys reflected on the wild events that had just transpired. They marveled at the fact that they had not only survived their first fight but had emerged victorious against Rahil, the college's most intimidating figure. Waleed, battered and bruised, struggled to hide a smile that betrayed his relief. Encouragement and camaraderie filled the room as they reassured him, 'Dude, you stood your ground against Rahil! He's like the scariest guy around here.' With those words, they warmly welcomed Waleed into their secret sanctuary, extracting a promise from him to keep their haven a secret.

During a light-hearted exchange, Waleed, still unfamiliar with the hideout's peculiar name, asked about its origin. Engaging in playful banter, the boys teased one another, until Waleed jokingly suggested, 'Maybe kastoori birds used to hang out here or something, but you know there is another Kastoor Penj in that mountain up there.' The comment unexpectedly sparked excitement in Burhan, who exclaimed,

'Finally someone who knows about these birds! Waleed, my friend, you're officially the smartest one in our group. You're gonna help us class up this joint!'

Amidst laughter and jests, Shahid couldn't resist warning Waleed, 'Be careful spending too much time with Burhan; your intelligence might dwindle faster than you can say "kastoori birds".' They all shared a good-natured laugh, aware that there was some truth to the jest. Waleed almost began to share the story of how Burhan had helped him Burhan signaled him with his eyes not to share that and Waleed obliged, the reason being Burhan was a shy person and never liked to be the center of attention.

The boys continued to chat, and Waleed began to open up. He shared his background, his village, and his dreams of pursuing education in the city. It was clear that Waleed was a bit out of place, but Abrar, Burhan, and Shahid didn't let that deter them. Instead, they tried to include him in their conversations, joking and laughing like old friends. As days turned into weeks, Waleed began to find his place among the trio. Despite their initial differences, a bond was forming that transcended backgrounds and appearances. They realized that underneath the surface, they shared the same aspirations, fears, and dreams. They welcomed Waleed into their group, showing him around the campus, helping him with studies, and even inviting him to their homes. The mismatch between Waleed and his new friends only seemed to highlight their good-hearted nature. They never made him feel like an outsider or made fun of his accent. Instead, they celebrated his uniqueness and encouraged him to be himself.

One afternoon, as they sat at Kastoor Penj, Waleed looked around at his new friends and couldn't help but smile. They were a group of misfits who had formed an unbreakable bond, bound by their shared experiences and the genuine care they had for each other. And so, amidst the laughter, late-night study sessions, and the occasional disagreements, their friendship blossomed. The unlikely quartet proved that true friendships are not based on appearances or backgrounds, but on the genuine connection that comes from understanding, acceptance, and the willingness to stand by each other through thick and thin.

As the weeks went by, the bond between Abrar, Burhan, Shahid, and Waleed continued to grow stronger. They became inseparable, spending their days together, sharing stories, and even developing their own inside jokes. Waleed's village accent, once so different, had become a part of their daily conversations, something that brought smiles and laughter.

One evening, as they were sitting by the campus, Waleed's smile seemed a bit dimmer. Abrar noticed the change and asked, 'Hey, what's on your mind?' Waleed sighed, looking out at the water.

'I don't know, guys. Lately, I have been feeling homesick. I miss my village, my mother, everything.'

Burhan put his arm around Waleed's shoulder, offering comfort. 'We understand, Waleed. It's natural to miss home. But, hey, how about we do something about it? How about a road trip, we can go to your village and also do some sightseeing, I always wanted to Wular lake?'

Shahid's eyes lit up with excitement. 'Yeah! We could go for a few days. What do you think Waleed?'

Waleed looked surprised and touched by their suggestion. 'You guys would really do that?'

Abrar grinned. 'Absolutely! We're your friends, Waleed.'

And just like that, a plan was set in motion. The boys spent the next few days planning for their unexpected road trip. They packed their bags, gathered snacks, and borrowed the car from Shahid's Uncle. Their excitement was contagious, and even Waleed's homesickness started to give way to anticipation.

As the car rolled out of Srinagar and onto the road that led to Waleed's village, the atmosphere was charged with excitement. The landscape changed from bustling city streets to scenic mountains, where lush green trees stretched out as far as the eye could see. Along the way, they made pit stops at roadside vendors, munching on local snacks and taking goofy pictures against breathtaking natural backdrops. The journey itself was becoming a treasure trove of memories. They sang songs, shared anecdotes, and created their own adventure playlist.

Finally, after hours on the road, they reached Waleed's village in Pattan. The picturesque beauty of the place was enchanting – rolling hills, quaint houses, and the warmth of a tight-knit community. Waleed's eyes glistened as he showed them around, sharing stories from his childhood and introducing them to his neighbors. The boys spent their days exploring the village, meeting Waleed's family, and immersing themselves in the rural life they had only heard about.

They plucked fresh fruit from orchards, shared meals with villagers, and even joined in a local festival, dancing to the tunes of traditional songs. On the last evening of their trip, as they sat under the stars, Waleed turned to his friends and said, 'Thank you, guys. This trip meant the world to me. You made me feel at home even when I was away from it.'

Burhan smiled, clinking his soda can against Waleed's. 'You are now part of us, now.'

Shahid nodded in agreement. 'Exactly. No matter where we come from, we've created a brotherhood right here.'

Abrar chuckled. 'And besides, we are always looking for excuses for road trips.'

As they headed back to Srinagar, Waleed's homesickness had transformed into a sense of belonging – to a group of friends who had welcomed him into their lives and hearts, ready to create memories together, no matter where the road took them.

As their road trip ended and they returned to their routine in Srinagar, the memories of their adventure lingered. The laughter, the shared moments, and the newfound understanding of each other's backgrounds had strengthened their bond in a way they never thought possible.

As a few days passed, and a new excitement filled the air as Shahid approached his friends one day with a grin on his face. 'Hey, guys, I've got some news! My cousin's getting married next month, and all of you and your families are invited!'

Abrar's eyes lit up. 'Which cousin? Is it Shabbir Bhai? Oh, I love that guy, he is the best.'

Burhan nodded in agreement. 'Absolutely, Shabbir bhai is the best.'

Waleed was intrigued and asked, 'Really? I want to meet your cousin then and I'm curious to see the city weddings.'

Shahid excitedly said, 'Oh, you will love Shabbir Bhai, I call him master ji, coz he is a master at everything. He is a bodybuilder, a great writer, poet, he was first in NIIT engineering exams in whole Kashmir and plus, he has a sweet Royal Enfield 500 cc motorcycle.'

Burhan, 'Oh, yeah, he has even let me ride that bike, love that guy.'

As the days passed, the anticipation for Shabbir bhai's wedding grew. Shahid shared anecdotes of their childhood with his cousin, how they used to explore the city together, and how Shabbir bhai had a knack for turning even the mundane into an exciting adventure.

# Chapter 3
# The Lost Parental Love

Burhan's childhood had been marred by the absence of his parents. They lived far away in Dubai and London, and he would only see them briefly once every two years when they visited Kashmir. These encounters were filled with superficial interactions, as his parents busied themselves with relatives and property investments. Burhan's aunt and uncle, sensing an opportunity, showered him with affection in the presence of his parents, while greedily seeking financial support from them. Burhan understood the manipulative game they played, but he kept this knowledge hidden from his unsuspecting parents, aware that revealing the truth would only lead to turmoil.

It was during Burhan's first year of college that his father, Wajahat, arrived in Kashmir with his new wife, Oksana, a middle-aged woman from Ukraine whom he had met while working at an engineering consulting firm. Burhan harbored mixed feelings towards Oksana, resenting her presence for various reasons.

However, he couldn't help but notice the genuine happiness radiating from his father's smile—a sight he hadn't witnessed in a long time.

Wajahat and Oksana spent just one night at Burhan's aunt's house before making plans to check into a hotel nestled in the mountains. Eager to showcase the beauty of Kashmir to his new wife, Wajahat seemed more interested in being a chauffeur and tour guide than spending quality time with his son. Oksana, hopeful for a complete family experience, urged Burhan to accompany them on their excursions to places like Gulmarg, Sonamarg, and other destinations on their itinerary. Though reluctant, Burhan politely declined, aware that his presence would only serve as a façade of familial harmony. He gave an excuse that he must be back to attend a wedding.

Oksana, disappointed by Burhan's refusal, approached Wajahat and engaged in a whispered conversation. Burhan observed his father's sigh of resignation before he reluctantly agreed to convince Burhan to join them, he promised Burhan they will be back before the wedding. With the car packed with luggage, the trio embarked on their journey to the mountains, where Oksana found herself enchanted by the breathtaking beauty of Kashmir. The rivers, the lush sea of trees, and the majestic glaciers left her in awe.

Curious about the sparse tourist presence, Oksana turned to Wajahat and asked why such a magnificent place remained relatively undiscovered. He replied with a hint of melancholy, 'This land was once home to saints, then many kings ruled over us, and now we are ruled by a country. Although no one could make us really part of them. The people of Kashmir have endured countless struggles. It used to be quite famous before the 90's, home to many Bollywood movies but after the Tehreek people were scared to come here and years after that Kashmir just became famous for its conflict and with time people just forgot about its beauty.' Meanwhile, Burhan sat in the backseat, silently messaging his friends about his current whereabouts—Pahalgam, with his father and his new wife.

As they drove deeper into the mountains, the scenery transformed into a captivating tapestry of nature's wonders. The air grew crisper, carrying the scent of pine trees. Burhan couldn't help but marvel at the idyllic surroundings, appreciating the beauty that had captivated Oksana. However, beneath his composed exterior, he carried the weight of unspoken truths, the burden of a fractured family dynamic, and the ever-present longing for genuine connection.

Oksana noticed everyone especially the kids staring at her and trying to talk to her, even though there were other tourists around, they seemed to be drawn to her. She asked the same to Wajahat who dismissed the question by answering, they are just curious, but Burhan chimmed in, 'It's because you are white, unfortunately the people in Kashmir, even the people in the whole Indian subcontinent have tendency to love white skin.'

Oksana, finding it weird looked out of car window, and jokingly replied, 'Haha, well, I guess I'm just adding a bit of variety to their day then.'

Burhan's childhood had been marked by the lingering echoes of his parents' turbulent relationship. The fights and arguments that reverberated through the walls of their home left an indelible mark on his young mind. Witnessing the discord between his mother and father had instilled in him a deep sense of unease and an aversion to anything that resembled love.

Burhan's parents, Wajahat, and Sana had once been deeply in love, but their marriage had become a battlefield of resentment and bitterness. Their fiery exchanges escalated over time, leaving their son caught in the crossfire. Their shouts and tears echoed through the hallways, painting a picture of a broken home. The impact on Burhan was profound, shaping his perception of love and relationships.

For years, Burhan had yearned for his parents to reconcile, to witness their affectionate gestures and genuine connection. Yet, their visits to Kashmir only reinforced the rift that had grown between them. Their time together was spent engrossed in external distractions, leaving little room for emotional intimacy or healing. Now, with his father's newfound love, Oksana, in the picture, Burhan found himself grappling with a strange mix of emotions.

Burhan's mind was flooded with memories of the fights between his parents, their bitter arguments tearing apart the fabric of their once harmonious home. The clashes had taken a toll on his young heart, leaving him scarred and apprehensive about the notion of love. He had become accustomed to the painful cycle of disappointment and resentment that hung heavy in the air whenever his parents were together.

Though he had not been a witness to their arguments for some time now, the wounds they had inflicted still throbbed within him. The scars left by his parents' tumultuous relationship ran deep, etching a permanent imprint on his understanding of love and its fragility. Burhan had learned to withdraw, shielding himself from the vulnerability that came with opening his heart to another.

However, the emergence of Oksana in his father's life brought a strange mix of emotions to the surface. On one hand, Burhan was relieved to witness his father's genuine happiness after a prolonged period of turmoil. For the first time in years, Wajahat's eyes sparkled with a sense of contentment that had long eluded him.

But on the other hand, seeing his father shower affection on another woman felt like a betrayal to Burhan, intensifying the void left by his parents' failed relationship.

Burhan grappled with conflicting emotions as he pondered the complex dynamics unfolding before him. He felt a profound sense of confusion, torn between wanting his father's happiness and the ache of his own unfulfilled desires for a reconciled family. The presence of Oksana seemed to magnify the void left by his mother, intensifying his longing for a renewed bond between his parents.

As the car continued its ascent through the winding mountain roads, Burhan's gaze shifted between the changing landscape and the interaction between his father and Oksana. Their conversations, filled with shared laughter and stolen glances, painted a picture of a love that was foreign yet undeniable. Burhan couldn't help but feel like an outsider, an intruder in their newfound happiness.

Burhan's hesitance to accompany his father and Oksana on their exploration of the breathtaking Kashmiri vistas stemmed from his desire to protect himself from the potential heartbreak of being an observer in their blossoming relationship. He feared becoming a mere shadow in their world, a constant reminder of the fractured family that had brought them together. As Burhan's father, Wajahat, and Oksana settled into their hotel room, the tranquility of the mountain resort embraced them. The crisp air and panoramic views were a stark contrast to the bustling city life they had left behind. But amidst the serenity, Burhan's phone buzzed, breaking the stillness of the moment. It was his mother calling.

Burhan's heart skipped a beat as he answered the call, his voice betraying a mix of anticipation and apprehension. It had been weeks since he last heard from his mother, their relationship strained by the bitter memories that lingered between them. Although he missed her, he couldn't shake off the weight of their past conflicts. His mother's voice, tinged with both concern and curiosity, filled the line. She greeted Burhan with a tenderness that he hadn't heard in a long time. In her carefully chosen words, she subtly probed about Oksana. Burhan sensed the underlying motive in her questions, a desire to understand the woman who had captured his father's heart.

Burhan hung up the phone, his mind awash with conflicting emotions. He couldn't help but question the intentions behind his mother's call, wondering if her genuine concern for his happiness was tainted by an ulterior motive. The weight of his parents' fractured relationship bore down on him, intensifying his struggle to find his own path amidst their tangled history.

In the midst of the breathtaking mountains, Burhan felt the weight of responsibility and the pull of conflicting loyalties. The tranquility of the surroundings served as a backdrop to his inner turmoil, urging him to confront the complexities of his past and carve out a future defined by his own choices.

During their stay at the mountain resort, Burhan found himself torn between the desire to spend quality time with his father and the ever-present weight of his own inner turmoil. Despite his initial reluctance, he had agreed to accompany

Wajahat and Oksana on their explorations of the scenic Kashmiri landscape.

For four days, Burhan embarked on an adventure alongside his father and Oksana, visiting picturesque locations like Gulmarg, Sonamarg, and the enchanting Dal Lake. The natural beauty that surrounded them seemed to cast a spell on Oksana, who marveled at the sights with wide-eyed wonder. Meanwhile, Burhan observed his father's eagerness to please his new wife, acting as her chauffeur and guide, rather than taking the opportunity to bond with his son.

In the evenings, as the trio returned to their hotel room, Burhan found solace in the silence of his thoughts. One particular night, feeling restless and burdened by the weight of his emotions, he stepped out onto the balcony overlooking the mist-covered valley. The crisp mountain air filled his lungs, but something was missing. It was during that moment of vulnerability that Burhan noticed one of the hotel's housekeeping staff taking a break nearby. The staff member, a seasoned individual with weathered features and a distant gaze, sat in solitude, puffing on a cigarette. The wisps of smoke swirled around him, creating an ethereal ambiance.

Curiosity piqued, Burhan approached the staff member and struck up a conversation. Burhan asked the staff member jokingly, 'Do you find yourself lucky working in such a beautiful place, and surrounded by these beautiful mountains and the sounds of these majestic rivers.' The staff member paused and with a sigh replied,

'Unfortunately we humans are ungrateful. I think we may get sick of the actual heaven, given enough time.' In the intimate exchange, the staff member shared stories of the hardships of life, and the solace he found in a simple cigarette.

Intrigued by this sense of escapism, Burhan hesitantly accepted the offer when the staff member offered him a cigarette of his own.

Under the influence of a heady mix of curiosity, rebellion, and a desire to break free from the confines of his own internal struggles, Burhan took his first drag. The smoke danced in the night air, mingling with the secrets whispered by the mountains. In that moment, a newfound ritual began—a ritual that would provide both an escape from reality and a constant reminder of his own inner battles.

Burhan, caught in the delicate dance of self-discovery, found himself drawn to the allure of smoking. The act itself seemed to provide a temporary respite from the complexities that plagued his mind. Each inhale allowed him to momentarily suspend his worries, creating an illusion of control and liberation.

As the days passed, Burhan's clandestine but secret habit began to intertwine with his experiences in the mountains. The puffs of smoke became a familiar sight amidst the stunning landscapes, a private ritual shared only between him and the whispered secrets of nature. It was a bittersweet comfort, a dangerous coping mechanism veiled in the guise of temporary relief.

As the days passed by at the mountain resort, Burhan's time with his father and Oksana gradually came to an end. The fleeting moments of togetherness they shared amidst the picturesque backdrop of Kashmir would soon fade into memories.

After their five-day stay at the resort, the time came for Wajahat and Oksana to bid farewell to the breathtaking mountains and return to their respective lives. The morning of their departure arrived, and there was a palpable sense of finality in the air. Burhan watched as his father and Oksana packed their belongings, preparing to leave the hotel and embark on their journey back Dubai. The weight of their impending departure settled upon him, mingling with the remnants of his own inner conflicts.

As they said their goodbyes, Burhan couldn't help but feel a mix of emotions. On one hand, he yearned for a deeper connection with his father, a relationship that had been strained by distance and a lack of presence throughout his upbringing. On the other hand, he struggled to reconcile his feelings towards Oksana, his father's new wife, whose presence in their lives had triggered a wave of conflicting emotions.

Burhan's father and Oksana, unaware of the brewing turmoil within their son, expressed gratitude for his presence during their trip. They exchanged warm hugs and promised to stay in touch, their words carrying the weight of unspoken desires for a more connected future.

With a heavy heart, Burhan watched as his father and Oksana departed, disappearing into the winding roads that led away from the mountains. The silence that followed their departure enveloped him, leaving behind a sense of emptiness and the echo of unanswered questions.

Burhan took a deep breath, inhaling the crisp mountain air, letting it cleanse his thoughts and renew his resolve. The mountains whispered secrets of resilience and growth, urging him to embrace the challenges ahead and find his own path amidst the vastness of the world. Burhan turned away from the departing shadows and began his journey back to his own reality. The mountains would forever remain a part of him, etched in his memories and eternally intertwined with the intricate tapestry of his life. And as he stepped forward, the mountains whispered, carrying his hopes and dreams into the winds, knowing that one day, he would return to their embrace.

# Chapter 4
# The Wedding

On the day of the awaited wedding, the boys gathered at Shahid's house, checking and trying on the clothes they were planning to wear on the wedding. Waleed had volunteered to make traditional dresses (kurta Shalwar) for his friends. The boys marvelled at the vibrant colors and intricate designs of the clothes and thanked Waleed for this gift. Waleed couldn't help himself and felt a sense of pride and belonging among the group.

The wedding ceremonies in Kashmir last for around seven days and the celebrations are quite unique to the region unlike the northern India and Pakistan. The first day is preparation day called "Malimanz" attended by close family members followed by "Mehnzraat" which is like a rehearsal dinner followed by the main day of Baraat, the main feast which includes "Wazwaan", a staggering chain of twenty dishes served by the traditional chefs called "Waza". After the main reception, four more days of celebrations continue with more "Wazwaan".

As they made their way to the venue, laughter and playful banter filled the air, lifting Waleed's spirits and helping him forget the hardships he had faced in the past. At the venue, which was the house of the groom's family, the boys became immersed in the lively atmosphere. The music, dancing, and delicious food created an ambiance of joy and celebration. Waleed found himself being introduced to Shahid's relatives, who welcomed him warmly, making him feel like a part of the family.

Throughout the event, Burhan stole glances at the female cousins of Shahid, who looked resplendent in their traditional attire. His heart fluttered with admiration, and he longed to approach to one of them. Even after encouraged by Abrar, Burhan couldn't gather the courage to strike up a conversation with any of them.

Meanwhile, Abrar, ever mischievous, found himself enjoying the wedding festivities in his own unique way. He made everyone laugh with his witty remarks and light-hearted pranks. His infectious laughter and carefree nature created a sense of joy that permeated the air. Abrar found himself caught up in the excitement of meeting new people and flirting with Shahid's cousins. His charming demeanor and playful flattery earned him smiles and giggles from the girls, adding a touch of flirtation to the wedding.

As the night progressed, Waleed found himself immersed in the cultural richness of the wedding. He couldn't help but marvel at the vibrant traditions and the sense of unity that permeated the gathering. It was an experience unlike any other he had ever had, and he was grateful to be a part of it. It was not just a celebration of love and union but also a celebration of newfound friendships and the breaking of barriers that had kept him isolated for so long.

Shahid's cousin Shabbir is marrying the love of his life, they have been together since college and after considerable convincing of the families the day was finally here. The boys had gathered in the groom's room checking out his three-piece suit, he was planning to wear for the main event. Shabbir bhai playfully told the boys to get out of the room and gave them chores to do as he had to step out to the salon.

The boys, entrusted with their respective wedding duties, labored diligently to fulfil their obligations, their tasks led them to the guest rooms, where they had to arrange mattresses and blankets, ensuring a comfortable resting place for the attending guests. Stepping into the final room, however, an unexpected tableau unfurled before their eyes—a gathering of female cousins immersed in an enchanting display of dance and song. Momentarily halted by the intrusion, they paused, their faces etched with surprise, before resuming their melodic revelry. Shahid, undeterred, smiled warmly and gestured for them to continue, and to his delight, they obliged, harmoniously melding their cadences with the resonant beats of the "tumbakhnair," the traditional long drums. Thus, laughter and music intertwined, enveloping the household, and infusing every corner with the sheer joy of the moment. Burhan and Abrar joined Shahid in dancing while the others seamlessly blended into the revelry, Waleed, with his natural shyness, cheered them on, his smile infused with a hint of awkwardness as he chimed in with the verses he knew.

Suddenly, a piercing cry shattered the buoyant ambiance, emanating from the ground floor. The boys rushed downstairs, their footsteps echoing with urgency, only to find the mother of the groom succumbing to an overwhelming surge of emotion, her anguish reverberating through the air. A pall of despair descended upon the scene as tears cascaded down their faces, while the groom's father stood frozen in disbelief. Shahid, seeking answers amidst the tumultuous sea of emotions, pleaded the gathering, his voice filled with anguish, 'What has happened? Is everything all right?' His mother, her voice wracked with sorrow, wailed in response,

'They have taken my son! They have taken my little groom!' His other uncle ushers Shahid and Abrar to the side and informs them,

'Shabbir was shot. He is in the hospital, we need to leave.' The father of the groom is in shock and starts running towards the door. The mother gets up from the chair and beats her chest in mourning screaming, 'They have killed my little groom, they have killed my son.'

The boys hurriedly made their way to the hospital, their hearts heavy with dread. Upon arrival, they were met with a disheartening sight – the police had already descended upon the hospital, obstructing their path to see the patient. Shahid and his friends, their faces etched with worry, pleaded with the doctor for any scrap of information.

'We're still in shock, doctor,' Shahid's voice quivered, 'his wedding is scheduled for tomorrow. Please, tell us, is he going to be, OK?'

The doctor cast a somber gaze upon them, his eyes filled with the weight of sorrow. 'I'm afraid the situation is grave.' He sighed, his words dripping with sorrow.

'He sustained a gunshot wound to the abdomen, and the internal bleeding is severe. To be brutally honest, there's a very real chance he might not make it. We need you to wait in the waiting area.'

As the doctor's words hung in the air, a profound sense of despair settled over Shahid, and his friends, their hopes dimming as they faced the bleak uncertainty of the impending hours. The boys then approached the individuals who had brought Shabbir to the hospital. They were anxious to know the full story, and it was from my perspective that I listened intently as they recounted the harrowing events.

One of them began, 'There was an ongoing protest in the area, and things escalated quickly. The military, and police responded with force, indiscriminately firing at the crowd without any warning. Your cousin, Shabbir, had been on his way to the salon to get his haircut for the wedding when he got caught up in the chaos.'

He continued, 'It's astonishing, really. Shabbir didn't even realize he had been shot. He managed to cross the road, and it was only then that we realized the severity of his condition. Without wasting a moment, we lifted him onto our scooter, and rushed him here to the hospital.'

As the boys absorbed this shocking account, the gravity of the situation began to sink in, and they exchanged worried glances, realizing the turmoil that Shabbir had unwittingly become a part of on what should have been a joyous occasion.

Hours felt like agonizingly long days as they awaited news on Shabbir's condition. Time seemed to crawl by as they grappled with the cruel uncertainty of the situation. Every passing moment felt like an eternity as they prayed for a miracle.

Finally, after what seemed like an eternity, the doctor emerged from the surgery room. His expression was heavy with sorrow, and his eyes bore the weight of delivering devastating news. He approached Shahid, and his family, and with a heavy heart, he spoke the words that shattered their world.

'I'm so sorry,' the doctor's voice quivered. 'Despite our best efforts, we couldn't save him. Shabbir didn't survive.'

Abrar, Burhan, and Waleed, their hearts heavy with grief, stood resolutely by Shahid's side, lending their strength in this time of unbearable sorrow. Shahid, grappling with a tsunami of emotions, pondered the enormity of the situation. How would his mother, and fiancé e react when they learned of this tragic loss?

The hospital walls echoed with mournful cries, a chorus of anguish that mirrored the despair that had enshrouded the entirety of Kashmir. To the casual observer, the region's picturesque valleys, and snow-clad mountains might appear as an idyllic paradize, but to the locals, it was a hell masquerading as heaven.

A month had passed, yet the gaping wound of Shabbir's untimely demise still bled fresh in the hearts of those who loved him. Shahid, consumed by an abyss of grief, had not found the strength to return to college. Seeking refuge in the familiar embrace of his uncle's home, his family clung to the solace offered by practical assistance, and emotional support. However, the once-vibrant atmosphere of the household now felt tainted by sorrow, as if the very walls mourned alongside them. To provide some respite to the bereaved parents, the father of the bride, along with Shabbir's father and uncles, had taken up temporary residence. They shared their grief, their anger, and their unwavering determination to bring their son's killing to the forefront of public awareness. Conversations with local press were their battle cries for justice, their pleas echoing in the turbulent winds of Kashmir.

Shahid's circle of friends had rallied around him, offering unwavering support during this tumultuous time. On this day, they arrived En-masse, classmates included, each eager to stand by Shahid and his family. Together, they convened in the somber confines of Shahid's uncle's guest room, their collective grief weighing heavily in the air. It was a room that had once witnessed laughter and camaraderie, but now it served as a sanctuary for shared anguish. As the silence threatened to drown them, Iram, Shahid's sister, entered the room, her tentative greeting shattering the oppressive stillness. She quietly counted the visitors, her actions a subtle gesture of hospitality, as she prepared tea to ease their somber gathering. She counted around twenty people who very sitting on the carpeted floor, as is the norm in Kashmir, the guests had squeezed themselves to fit in that room. Among the guests was Samreen, a presence that had already captured Shahid's affections, a fact he had confided in his sister. With Iram's departure to the kitchen, the room remained in quiet contemplation, a collective heaviness settling over them.

As the minutes passed, condolences were tenderly offered to Shahid, their voices carrying the weight of shared sorrow. They mourned not only Shabbir's loss but also the grim state of affairs that had enveloped Kashmir. Samreen, with a compassionate look in her eyes, extended her support to Shahid, her words a soothing balm to his wounded heart. Shahid, grateful for their presence, expressed his thanks, his voice tinged with vulnerability.

In the midst of their shared sorrow, Shakir, one of Shahid's classmates, broached a topic that hung like a shadow over their futures. He revealed his intention to relocate to Dubai after completing his education, citing the rising insecurity in

Kashmir, the dearth of job opportunities, and the pervasive sense of hopelessness as the driving factors behind his decision. Waleed, the eternal optimist among them, scanned the room for dissent, but found none. The silence that followed was a collective acknowledgment of the harsh realities they faced, a stark contrast to the once-bright dreams they had held.

Amid their shared grief, a subtle transformation unfolded within Burhan, one of Shahid's closest friends. He had taken to openly smoking, a habit he had previously hidden from his friends. It was his way of seeking solace amidst the shared sorrow, a silent acknowledgment of the pain they all felt.

After a while, Iram returned with trays of tea, Samreen volunteered in assisting Iram in serving everyone. As Samreen handed a cup of tea to Shahid, their eyes locked for a fleeting moment, a connection forming between them that transcended words. Burhan, a keen observer, could not help but smile, witnessing the blossoming relationship between his friend and Samreen. As the guests prepared to depart, Samreen struck up a conversation with Iram. Their discussion, filled with shared laughter and empathetic understanding, seemed to stretch on for a considerable time. Shahid watched anxiously as the friendship between his sister and Samreen deepened, and before parting ways, they exchanged phone numbers, marking the beginning of a new and promising chapter in their lives.

# Chapter 5
# The Fall

Five months had passed since the loss of Shahid's cousin, Shabbir. The boys found themselves gathered in Burhan's aunt's house, seeking solace in the familiar distraction of video games. Their laughter echoed through the room, momentarily overshadowing the heavy atmosphere that lingered in the air.

Then, a sudden, aggressive knock at the door sent shockwaves through their gaming session, instantly putting a halt to their frenzied play. Burhan's aunt made her entrance, her displeasure with their presence thinly veiled. With a touch of coldness in her voice, she addressed Burhan, reminding him of their previous conversation, 'Burhan, don't forget to call your father tonight. You understand what we discussed.'

Burhan exchanged a glance with his friends, their attempts to appear innocent falling short as nervous smiles played upon their lips. As his aunt departed, Shahid couldn't help but express his true feelings. 'I don't like her,' he confessed, the words escaping his lips with a mix of relief and apprehension.

Abrar, taken aback by Shahid's candor, looked at him and then at Burhan, surprised that Shahid had vocalized what they all felt. Burhan paused for a moment before bursting into laughter. 'Yeah, me too,' he admitted, joining in Shahid's sentiment.

Abrar, relieved by Burhan's response, chuckled and agreed, 'Yes, I hate that woman.'

Burhan's laughter subsided, and he fixed his gaze on Abrar. 'Hate is a strong word,' he remarked, a serious undertone coloring his words. Abrar's laughter faltered, his face reflecting a tinge of regret, but before he could apologize, Burhan's laughter resumed. It was all a jest, a moment of light-heartedness amidst their shared frustrations.

'I hate her too,' he finally confessed, relieving Abrar from any lingering guilt.

Their laughter enveloped the room once more as they resumed their game, momentarily setting aside their troubles. Amidst the joyous chaos, Shahid's phone rang, and he excused himself, stepping out to answer the call. It was Samreen, the first time they were speaking directly to each other.

Samreen asked, 'How have you been, Shahid?'

Shahid's voice carried a mixture of happiness and gratitude as he replied, 'I am OK.'

The conversation drifted towards their plans for the next day, and Shahid, barely containing his excitement, proposed meeting for tea or coffee. Samreen agreed, and they settled on a cafe in the city. Returning to Burhan's room, Shahid could not contain his elation, his radiant smile captivating his friends. He shared the details of his conversation, and Burhan and Abrar, unable to believe the turn of events, embraced him tightly, dancing in jubilation.

After the boys had left the house, and he made his way to his room, Burhan unintentionally overheard a tense conversation between his aunt and uncle.

Aunt Shazia with her voice laced with exasperation shouting, 'I simply can't understand how you allowed Burhan to bring those friends of his into our home. You're aware of how strongly I object to it.'

Uncle Hamid, ever the mediator, endeavored to maintain a sense of calm during this familial tempest, 'Shazia, please, let's not let this escalate further. They're just youngsters, enjoying themselves. What harm could there be?'

However, Aunt Shazia's resolve remained unwavering, her stance unyielding, 'Listen, I understand his parents don't want him with them, and I don't mind him being here in MY house but I draw a line, if he brings company to our house, this is not a hotel.'

Uncle Hamid, compelled to defend his nephew, put forth his perspective, 'Shazia, they have been friends since they were kids.'

Aunt Shazia's frustration reached its peak, her words emerging as a final plea, 'It's easy for you to say, Hamid. You don't witness their unruly behavior as I do. And just to remind you, we have a young daughter here in this house.'

In a gesture of compromise, Uncle Hamid sought common ground, 'Very well, we'll have a conversation with Burhan about this. But let us not magnify this issue beyond proportion. They are kids!'

As the weight of his aunt's words settled upon Burhan's shoulders, he ascended the stairs to his room, deep in contemplation. To clear his mind, he instinctively reached into his pocket and pulled out a cigarette, longing for a momentary escape. Positioning himself near the window, Burhan leaned out, allowing the smoke to dissipate into the open air. His hand shielded the lingering scent from permeating his room, masking the evidence of his secret habit. With each inhale, a fleeting sense of calm washed over him, temporarily easing the turmoil within.

Lost in his thoughts, Burhan stared into the distance, the faint glow of the cigarette illuminating his face. The smoke curled and danced on the gentle breeze, carrying away fragments of his worries as he sought solace in the ritualistic rhythm of smoking. With a heavy sigh, he pushed open the window, allowing the cool evening air to circulate within the room, dissipating any remnants of smoke that may linger. The scent of his secret dissipated along with it, leaving behind only the faintest trace of his inner struggle.

Burhan felt a restlessness stirring within him as he decided to take a walk, hoping to escape the turmoil of his current circumstances. He walked for a while till he reached near the boulevard of Dal Lake. He reached for his phone and dialed his father's number, longing for a comforting voice to guide him through his troubles. However, his anticipation was met with disappointment as his father's new wife, Oksana, answered the call, informing him that his father was not home and advising him to call later.

Seeking solace, Burhan dialed his mother's number next, but she did not answer. The silence on the other end of the line deepened his sense of vulnerability.

Determined to find a temporary refuge, he continued walking until he reached the tranquil shores of the nearby lake. There, he sat alone, his thoughts swirling amidst the calmness of the surroundings.

Unbeknownst to Burhan, two figures strolling along the lake noticed him from a distance. As they drew closer, Burhan recognized them as his college mates Ather and Ubaid.

Ather had a mature appearance that belied his youth. His curly black hair and pale skin gave him an artistic flair, but his sunken eyes told another story. Dark circles ringed his eyes, hinting at experiences and weariness beyond his years. There was a haunted look in his gaze, as if he was staring into an abyss within himself. In contrast, Ubaid's slender build was exaggerated to an unhealthy extreme. He was thin to the point of looking skeletal, his sharp features accentuated by the lack of flesh on his face. His wrists protruded like fragile twigs, and he moved with the slow deliberate steps of someone lacking in energy.

Ather recognized Burhan as a fellow student from their college and his eyes lit up with a glimmer of curiosity. He urged Ubaid to continue his way before approaching Burhan himself. Athar settled beside Burhan, initiating a conversation with a friendly smile. 'Hey, aren't you from our college? I'm your senior,' he began, trying to ease Burhan's unease. Burhan replied politely, acknowledging their connection. As Athar pulled out a cigarette, its pungent aroma hinting at something more than tobacco, he extended an offer to Burhan. Initially declining, Burhan found himself swayed by Athar's persistence and reluctantly accepted the cigarette.

With cautious hesitation, Burhan took a drag, feeling a tickle in his throat. Athar, taking a puff himself, spoke about the perceived benefits of marijuana over cigarettes, suggesting that Burhan should consider making the switch. Burhan chuckled, dismissing the notion, affirming his loyalty to traditional cigarettes.

Sensing Burhan's resistance, Athar let the matter rest, bidding him farewell before departing.

In the days that followed, Burhan and Athar found themselves crossing paths more frequently on campus. Athar's friendly demeanor and charismatic nature began to draw Burhan into his orbit. They laughed, shared jokes, and engaged in conversations that revolved around the pursuit of pleasure and the allure of experimentation. Slowly, Burhan found himself succumbing to the influence of Athar's carefree spirit.

As their friendship deepened, Burhan started to smoke marijuana more frequently, seeking solace in its temporary relief from the weight of his troubles. Burhan's prior knowledge about the diverse types of marijuana was quite limited. He had never delved into the nuances of cannabis varieties. During his growing friendship with Athar, he began to discover the intriguing world of cannabis. One day, Athar decided to share his knowledge, shedding light on the distinct forms of marijuana.

'Burhan,' Athar began, 'there's actually a lot to know about marijuana. For instance, there's "Charas", a potent form of cannabis. It's essentially the concentrated oil extracted from the flower buds of the cannabis plant. You can either smoke it directly or mix it with tobacco to enhance the experience. The most potent "Charas" is called ittar.'

Burhan listened intently; his curiosity piqued. Athar continued, 'Then there's 'Ganja', another popular variant. It's made from the dried buds of the cannabis plant.'

As Athar elaborated, Burhan found himself fascinated by the intricacies of cannabis culture, a world he had previously known little about.

One fateful day, after the conclusion of their classes, Athar approached Burhan with a glint of mischief dancing in his eyes. 'Hey, Burhan, I know a place where we can have some real fun,' he exclaimed, his voice brimming with excitement.

Burhan's curiosity sparked anew, a blend of apprehension and eagerness enveloping him. Athar's words hung in the air, tempting him to break free from the shackles of his everyday life. It was a tantalizing offer, one that hinted at an escape from his worries, but also carried a sense of uncertainty.

Intrigued, Burhan hesitated for a moment before asking, 'What kind of fun?'

Ather leaned in closer and whispered, 'I'm talking about a secret drug heaven. It's a place where many of my friends gather to enjoy getting high without anyone knowing. It's an escape from the mundane and a gateway to an entirely different world.'

Burhan's curiosity piqued, but he felt a mix of apprehension and intrigue. He had heard stories of drug heavens and the devastating consequences it could bring. However, the allure of experiencing something new and exciting gnawed at him.

'I don't know, Ather,' Burhan hesitated, 'I've never done anything like that before.'

Ather shrugged nonchalantly. 'It's OK, Burhan. I don't want to force you. Just think of it as trying something different, stepping out of your comfort zone. You don't have to do anything you're uncomfortable with.' Burhan contemplated the offer. The idea of experiencing an escape from his problems, even just temporarily, held a certain allure.

He weighed the risks and rewards in his mind, battling with his own inner demons.

Finally, in the depths of the night, Burhan quietly followed Ather to a hidden, enigmatic location far from the prying eyes of the world. The moment they stepped into the dimly lit space, a visceral assault of sensations overwhelmed Burhan's senses. The pungent aroma of marijuana hung heavy in the air, shrouding the room in an intoxicating haze. Here, a group of individuals from all walks of life had converged, each seeking their own form of solace and oblivion through the allure of substances.

As Burhan wandered through the labyrinthine corridors of this clandestine world, he was transported to realms he had never known. Music echoed all around, with some rooms resonating to the soulful tunes of Nusrat Fateh Ali Khan's sufi melodies, while others pulsed with the hypnotic beats of psychedelic trance. It was an intoxicating symphony that seemed to beckon him further into the unknown.

In the upper reaches of the building, Burhan encountered Ubaid, the enigmatic slender figure always draped in winter clothing even amidst scorching temperatures. Ubaid extended a hand bearing a pinch of white powder, urging Burhan to partake. Burhan hesitated for a fleeting moment, his curiosity warring with his reservations. Yet, he succumbed to the allure of the unknown and, with a snort, unleashed a firestorm in his senses. It was as if a legion of fiery ants had invaded his brain, an electrifying sensation that should have jolted him awake, yet paradoxically, his limbs relaxed into a tranquil languor.

Minutes slipped away as Burhan found himself curled up in a remote corner, the world around him a surreal tapestry of emotions and sensations. It was here that Ather came to his side, offering a joint of marijuana that seamlessly melded with his euphoric high. In that moment, amidst the warmth and haze, Burhan experienced an unfamiliar sense of contentment, cocooned in a blanket that felt like the softest embrace the world had to offer.

As the night progressed, Burhan found himself caught up in a whirlwind of emotions. The drugs offered him an escape from his inner turmoil, erasing the worries and anxieties that burdened him. In that moment, he felt a sense of freedom and liberation, something he hadn't experienced before.

Unbeknownst to Burhan, Ather had a hidden agenda. You see, he was recruiter for new customers, and he preferred educated rich young men to the poor, homeless drug addicts. Much easier to manage and little to no mess to clean. Ather slowly exploited Burhan's vulnerability, gradually pushing him towards more potent substances. Under the guise of friendship, Ather would introduce Burhan to drugs that would slowly consume his life, turning him into a mere shadow of his former self.

The motive was money, and Burhan was good for it, he paid right away and never made Ather wait but similar to any other business, Ather was getting greedy, and he kept increasing the price of the drugs, always with some new excuse of how difficult it was getting to obtain these drugs. As weeks turned into months, Burhan's visits to the secret drug haven became more frequent. The line between experimentation and addiction blurred, and Burhan found himself entangled in a web he couldn't escape.

Burhan's fascination with drugs had slowly taken hold of him, and he couldn't help but share his newfound experience with his closest friends, Abrar, Shahid, and Waleed. He knew he cannot share his experience of drugs with his friends, but he believed that they, too, would find solace and joy in the world of "Charas". With excitement brewing within him, Burhan devised a plan to introduce his friends to the drug in a picturesque mountain resort.

The four friends embarked on a weekend getaway, leaving behind the hustle and bustle of their daily lives. As they reached the serene mountain resort, Burhan unveiled his intentions, inviting them to try Marijuana together. Intrigued by the idea of exploring new experiences, Shahid, Abrar, and Waleed agreed to join in with a mix of curiosity and apprehension.

Under the starry night sky, the friends sat around a crackling bonfire, passing a joint among themselves. As the smoke enveloped their senses, their laughter became infectious, and funny stories flowed effortlessly. They reveled in the euphoria, sharing their innermost thoughts and connecting on a deeper level. Burhan was also snorting something every time he went to the toilet and Waleed almost noticed it but didn't pursue his intuition.

Burhan couldn't help but share his newfound knowledge about cannabis with his close friends. As they settled in for a relaxed evening, he eagerly began discussing the various forms of marijuana they could explore.

'Hey, guys,' Burhan said, a playful grin on his face. 'Did you know there are different types of marijuana? What we're smoking right now is called "Charas". It's the concentrated oil extracted from the flower buds of the cannabis plant. Mixing it with tobacco can give you a unique experience.'

Shahid, Abrar, and Waleed exchanged intrigued glances. Shahid, inquisitive, asked Burhan, 'When did you start smoking marijuana, and how do you know so much about this Charas?'

Burhan replied defensively, 'Well, I have some other friends besides you guys, and this helps me relax and ease my anxiety.'

Abrar, Shahid, and Waleed were open to trying something new, especially in this laid-back setting. They didn't think too much of it and continued to smoke, passing the joint among them.

Burhan continued, 'Now, there's also Ganja, which is made from the dried buds of the cannabis plant. It's the most common form of marijuana in the world.'

As the night progressed and the effects of the drug began to fade, Burhan reached into his pocket and pulled out another joint. He held it out to his friends, a mischievous glint in his eyes. Shahid, Abrar, and Waleed happily accepted, and they spent the entire night laughing and sharing moments. For Burhan, everything seemed to slow down, and he felt an overwhelming happiness he hadn't experienced in a while.

The next morning, as everyone prepared to trek the beautiful mountains, Burhan surprised them by taking out another joint. He looked at them mischievously and said, 'Let's get high first and then we can start our trek.'

Abrar looked at Burhan with concern and said, 'Burhan, we had an amazing time last night, but we need to be mindful. We don't want to fall into a pattern of dependency. Let's cherish this experience as a special occasion and not let it consume us.'

Shahid added in a gentle yet firm tone, 'I told Samreen what we did, and she's really upset with me. She made me promise not to do this again.'

Waleed, who had been quietly observing, nodded in agreement. 'I'm feeling a bit guilty from yesterday, and I don't want to do it again.'

Burhan felt a pang of disappointment, as all he wanted was to recreate the happiness he had felt the previous night. However, he respected his friends' concerns and agreed to put the joint away. He told them to get ready, assuring them that he would join them shortly.

# Chapter 6 Rebirth

Abrar and Waleed juggled their college responsibilities and part-time jobs, their attention inadvertently shifted away from Burhan. Lost in their own worlds, they failed to notice the subtle signs of Burhan's continuing struggle with addiction. Shahid was also blissfully caught up in the euphoria of his new relationship.

Spending most of his time with Samreen, he unintentionally distanced himself from the once inseparable bond he shared with Burhan. The few times they crossed paths, Burhan put on a facade, concealing the depths of his addiction, and painting a picture of false normalcy.

They noticed a change in Burhan's behavior. He had become distant, unreliable, and his once infectious laughter faded away. Concerned for their friend, they tried to reach out, but Burhan evaded their inquiries, hiding his addiction behind a facade of secrecy and denial.

The city had been grappling with a surge in drug-related issues, with a noticeable increase in cases of drug overdoses. Despite efforts to curb the problem, the prevalence of narcotics continued to rise unabated. It was a concerning trend that was taking a toll on the youth of Srinagar.

A particularly troubling transformation was occurring among the city's young men, especially boys. They seemed to be evolving into something of a new breed: pseudo rap-loving gangsters. These young individuals would often be found driving aimlessly around the city, their senses clouded by the effects of drugs.

What was once a serene and culturally rich valley was now witnessing a darker, more turbulent side of its youth.

The consequences of this shift were dire. High on drugs, these young men would occasionally engage in violent confrontations with one another. What started as petty disputes escalated into physical altercations, leaving behind serious injuries and, tragically, even deaths. It was a stark contrast to the harmony and tranquility that the city had once been known for.

One evening, as the sun began to set Abrar, and Waleed met at their favorite spot, Kastoor Penj, to exchange notes and prepare for the exams. It had been a while since they had gathered there together, and there was a mixture of anticipation and concern in the air. They missed Burhan's presence but lately he wasn't responding to their calls and texts. As they settled down, Abrar noticed a peculiar smell lingering in the air. His eyes narrowed, and he followed the scent to its source—Burhan, who seemed distant and lost in his own world. Abrar's heart sank as he realized that Burhan was using drugs right there at their sacred meeting place.

Abrar couldn't bear the weight of this discovery alone. With a heavy heart, he gathered Waleed, and led them to where Burhan sat, lost in the haze of addiction. The mixture of disappointment, anger, and concern swirled within Abrar as he confronted his friend.

'Burhan, what are you doing?' Abrar's voice trembled with a mix of emotions.

Burhan's eyes widened as he realized he had been caught in the act. A veil of shame descended upon him, but he quickly gathered himself and responded with defensiveness. 'What am I doing? Nothing, just came to relax.'

Abrar replied screaming, 'What kind of relaxation is this, you been avoiding us for this…we didn't mind you smoking weed but now you are using these hard drugs? What the hell?'

Burhan struggling with word but visibly upset screamed, 'And what about all of you? You think you're such great friends? You abandoned me when I needed you the most!'

Waleed stepped forward; his voice filled with sorrow. 'Burhan, we have been trying to call you, you never answer these days.'

Abrar interviewed as he was now getting more concerned after noticing Burhan was slurring through words. 'What kind of drugs are you using, you are looking ill.'

Burhan whispered, 'It's only Marijuana.'

Abrar: 'Don't lie to me, you were injecting something in your arm man. Just now.'

Burhan trying to muster his wits to answer, 'Listen, just let me be, it's none of your business anyway to know what drugs I am using.'

Abrar now raging replied, 'Even if I have to call your parents from fucking UK and Dubai and I have to drag them here to fix you I will do that, and wait till I share this with Shahid.'

'Shahid is busy with his new girlfriend as you are with your studies, just leave me alone.'

Burhan's eyes filled with tears, a mixture of frustration and guilt. He realized that he had placed the blame on his friends, trying to justify his addiction instead of facing the reality of his situation. The weight of his words and their impact hung heavy in the air.

Waleed knew his limits and being the rational person, he softly said, 'Burhan, we care about you. You should quit these drugs, we will support you.'

Burhan suddenly leapt up and walked away shouting, 'I don't want to change, I am good as I am, leave me be.'

Abrar and Waleed stood there exchanging glances of concern and watched Burhan walking away.

A few days passed by and the once-unbreakable bond between Burhan, Shahid, Abrar, and Waleed began to fray at the edges. The demands of adulthood were pulling them in different directions, and their paths were diverging. Burhan, who had once been the vibrant heart of their group and the driving force behind their adventures, had tragically become ensnared in the unforgiving grip of drug addiction. His life had taken a grim and desolate turn as he struggled to cope with the overwhelming weight of depression. To him, these drugs had become a desperate escape from a reality that had become too difficult to bear.

Despite their growing concerns and the widening chasm between them, Burhan's friends refused to give up on him. They kept reaching out, making countless calls and sending heartfelt messages in an attempt to pull their friend back from the abyss he was descending into. They knew that they were witnessing the unravelling of a cherished friendship, and they couldn't bear to see Burhan suffer alone.

They kept visiting Burhan's home, believing that a face-to-face conversation might be the key to breaking through the walls he had built around himself. However, whenever they arrived at Burhan's place, their efforts were met with an unexpected and disheartening response.

Every time they came to see Burhan, it was either Burhan's aunt with a hidden smile or Burhan's uncle with a genuine sadness, informing them that Burhan was not at home. It was clear that Burhan, in his desperate isolation, had taken the step of distancing himself for them. This were a stark indication of the lengths to which Burhan had gone to shield himself from the concern and intervention of those who cared about him. They were left with a growing sense of helplessness, unable to reach their friend and unsure of how to intervene in a situation that was becoming increasingly dire.

One evening, as the golden hues of the setting sun painted the room in a warm, amber glow, Burhan found himself trapped in a ritual that had become an inescapable part of his life. It was a ritual of despair, one that unfolded silently in the shadows, away from prying eyes. With each passing day, it became a mechanical routine, etched into his muscle memory like an insidious mantra. He waited patiently, the hours dragging on as he listened to the faint sounds of his family members retiring to their bedrooms, the night's curtain descending upon their day.

Finally, when the house was cloaked in the comforting shroud of darkness and silence, he took cautious steps towards his secret, concealed beneath his wardrobe. His fingers traced the edges of the hidden bag, fingers trembling with a mix of anticipation and dread. This bag held his escape, his salvation, and his curse.

Gently, he retrieved the bag, the cold touch of it sending a shiver down his spine. Inside lay a collection of syringes and vials, but not the ones you'd find at a pharmacy. These contained a perilous concoction of heroin mixed with morphine. It was a desperate attempt to chase a high, a fleeting moment of euphoria in a life otherwise shrouded in misery.

Burhan settled onto his bed, the faded covers the only witnesses to his secret torment. Slowly, he peeled the shirt from his arms, revealing a canvas of despair. His once-healthy limbs were now marred by a sinister tapestry of track marks, the scars of many injections marking the passage of time and the descent into addiction.

With practiced precision, he selected a syringe and began the delicate process of finding a suitable vein. It was a grim dance of self-destruction, the needle a cruel partner in a macabre waltz. As the contents of the syringe flowed into his veins, he felt the familiar rush of euphoria. It was a fragile high, a brief respite from the harsh realities that weighed him down.

Minutes turned into hours as he lay on his bed, lost in the embrace of the drug-induced reverie. His phone, a lifeline to a world he had left behind, beckoned to him. Fingers trembling, he navigated through a gallery of images, his heart aching at the sight of his friends' faces. The photographs were frozen moments in time, capturing the smiles and laughter that had once been his constant companions. In that fleeting instant, Burhan couldn't help but feel a surge of emotion, an overwhelming longing for the friends he had distanced himself from.

Yet, as the drug's grip began to loosen, a different emotion clawed at him—disgust. It crept over him like a cold, unforgiving wave, and he loathed what he had become, the weakness that had brought him to this point.

Summoning every ounce of courage he could muster, he pushed himself to his feet, a nauseating sensation washing over him. The bathroom beckoned like a sanctuary, a place to wash away not just the physical grime but the emotional filth that clung to him. After splashing his face with cold water, he stared at his reflection in the mirror. The hollow eyes that stared back at him were a stark reminder of the depths to which he had sunk. It was a moment of reckoning, a stark realization that he could no longer bear this burden alone.

With trembling hands and a heart heavy with remorse, he reached for his phone. It was time for a life-altering call.

With trembling hands, he dialed Abrar's number. His voice quivered as he spoke, 'Abrar, it's me, Burhan. I need to talk to you.'

Abrar, surprised and concerned, replied, 'Burhan? Is everything OK, what time is it?'

Tears welled up in Burhan's eyes as he confessed, 'Sorry to call you so late and No, Abrar, everything's not OK. I've messed up, big time. I'm sick of this life, of the drugs, and everything that I've become. I need your help.'

Abrar's heart ached for his friend. He understood that this was a cry for help, a plea for redemption. 'Burhan, we're here for you,' he assured him.

'Let's talk to Shahid and Waleed too. We'll figure this out together.'

With Burhan's consent, Abrar added Shahid and Waleed to the call. As the four friends gathered virtually, a somber silence hung in the air. Burhan, his voice laced with vulnerability, began to speak.

'Guys, I've messed up big time. I can't keep living like this, drowning myself in drugs. I've hurt myself, and all of you. I'm so sorry.'

Shahid's voice, filled with concern and compassion, replied, 'Burhan, we've missed you. We know we have been busy with our lived, but we are here for you. We'll help you through this.'

Waleed, his usual optimism shining through, added, 'Burhan, remember the good times we had? Plus, you have helped me so much, I am there for you always.'

Burhan sobbing, 'Thank you for not giving up on me, I'm going to seek help, guys. I want to change, and I'll do whatever it takes. Please forgive me.'

Burhan didn't waste a moment. After the call, he threw open his closet and pulled out the bag containing the remnants of his drug-related past. With each discarded pipe and every empty baggie that hit the trash, he felt a weight lift off his shoulders. It was a symbolic cleansing, a tangible declaration that he was done with that dark chapter of his life.

The days that followed were some of the most challenging Burhan had ever faced. Withdrawal symptoms gripped him with merciless intensity. He battled nausea, tremors, anxiety, and the relentless cravings that whispered in the back of his mind. The boys took turns staying with Burhan, offering comforting words, distraction, and unwavering support. They knew that he had to keep his struggle hidden from his aunt, uncle, and parents, who remained oblivious to his past actions.

Through the long nights and grueling days, they reminded Burhan of the brighter future that awaited him once he conquered his demons. They listened to his fears and reassured him that he was not alone in this battle.

As the midterm examinations loomed on the horizon, the boys found themselves caught in a whirlwind of textbooks, notes, and last-minute study sessions. The weight of academic responsibility pressed upon them, and they knew that success in these exams would mark the culmination of their college journey.

Burhan, in particular, faced a daunting challenge. His past struggles with addiction had cost him precious time and focus, leaving him with a significant academic backlog. But he was not alone in this endeavor. His loyal friends, Abrar, Shahid, and Waleed, rallied to his side with unwavering support. Late into the night, under the warm glow of study lamps, they poured over textbooks together. Waleed, the academic achiever, patiently explained complex concepts to Burhan, who was determined to catch up on missed coursework. Abrar, always reliable, quizzed him on important topics, ensuring he retained the knowledge. Shahid, balancing his own academic responsibilities made time to encourage and motivate Burhan when frustration threatened to overwhelm him.

They were gathered in Shahid's house and Shahid's room had become a hub of diligence and camaraderie. Study materials covered the coffee table, and mugs of strong coffee fueled their late-night sessions. Together, they study and memorized till the early hours of the morning.

In the days leading up to the midterm exams, as the pressure mounted and the revision sessions grew longer, the boys realized the importance of a good night's sleep before the big day. With their notes meticulously reviewed and everything practiced to perfection, they made a collective decision to disband temporarily and seek rest in the comfort of their respective homes.

As the midterm exams progressed, the four friends displayed remarkable dedication and confidence in their studies. They attended each exam with a sense of purpose, armed with their knowledge and preparedness. The first few exams passed smoothly, and their optimism grew with every passing day. They supported each other, reviewed notes together, and encouraged one another to do their best.

As the boys gathered in Shahid's cozy room, covered in textbooks and notes, their discussions often veered into light-hearted banter about their friend Shahid and his budding romance with Samreen. The topic never failed to bring a smile to their faces, providing a welcome break from their rigorous study sessions.

Abrar, with a mischievous grin, couldn't resist teasing Shahid. 'Hey, Shahid, you've been spending so much time with Samreen lately. Have you been really concentrating on midterms?'

Shahid, cheeks slightly flushed, defended himself with a chuckle. 'Come on, guys! You know I've got everything under control. Samreen understands the importance of exams. Plus, we study together sometimes.'

Abrar, always the voice of reason, chimed in, 'That's great, Shahid, as long as you strike a balance. Remember, we boys got to stand together, especially during these exams.'

Burhan, in a playful mood, decided to add his two cents. 'Shahid, I heard Samreen makes some killer chai. Maybe you should tell her to bring us a kettle of tea sometime.'

Laughter filled the room as they imagined the scenario. Amidst the jokes and camaraderie, it was evident that the bond between these friends remained strong, even as they navigated the changes in their lives.

# Chapter 7
# Worst News

It was the last day of midterm examinations, but there was a palpable sense of worry in the air. As the clock ticked closer to the start of the exam, Burhan had not yet arrived. Concern etched on their faces, Abrar, Shahid, and Waleed exchanged glances, silently hoping that Burhan would show up any moment. They knew that Burhan had been working hard to catch up on his studies after his struggle with drugs, and he had been making good progress.

As the minutes ticked away, the teacher in charge of the examination announced that the papers would be distributed soon. The anxiety in the room intensified, and the boys' exchanged whispers about Burhan's whereabouts. Shahid checked his phone for any messages or calls but found none. It was unlike Burhan to be late, especially on such an important day.

With a heavy heart and the fear of missing the exam weighing on them, the trio made a difficult decision. They decided to start the examination without Burhan. It was a painful choice, but they couldn't risk their own academic futures while hoping for his arrival. They knew that Burhan would understand their predicament. As they began the exam, their minds were divided between the questions on the paper and worries for their friend. They silently prayed that Burhan was safe and that he would find his way to them soon.

After the midterm examination concluded, the trio of Abrar, Shahid, and Waleed couldn't shake off their growing anxiety about Burhan's absence. Their concern for their friend had reached a new level. They decided to immediately call Burhan, hoping for an explanation. However, their repeated calls to his phone went unanswered, plunging them deeper into unease.

Desperate for any information, they even attempted to reach out to Burhan's aunt, she didn't know anything about his whereabouts. The gravity of the situation sank in as the boys realized that Burhan's own family had no idea of his whereabouts. Fear gnawed at their hearts, and their worry escalated. It was unlike Burhan to disappear like this, especially on such an important day.

The following day weighed heavily on the trio as they embarked on another round of searches for Burhan. They scoured every nook and cranny of the places they had frequented together, retracing their steps, hoping to stumble upon any clue that would lead them to their missing friend.

They made their way to Burhan's uncle and aunt's house. They knew that Burhan's uncle and aunt had been oblivious to his absence, assuming he was with his friends as usual. They needed to convince them of the gravity of the situation and urge them to take immediate action. They convinced Burhan's uncle to accompany them to the police station to file a missing person report.

As they were heading towards the police station, Burhan's uncle receives a devastating phone call that shattered their world. Burhan had been found dead. Shock and disbelief coursed through his face as he struggled to comprehend the unimaginable loss. The boys struggled to maintain their composure, but the news had shaken them to their core. Gathering themselves, they hurried to the location where Burhan's life had been tragically cut short. It was a police officer who had called him and informed him that Burhan's body was found near the Jhelum riverbank.

They walk towards the scene filled hundreds of people gathered around trying to understand what was going on. The boys moved past the crowd and came near the crime scene, although the police had cordoned the area. The air was heavy with sorrow as they approached the scene, their hearts pounding with a mix of grief and apprehension. The police had begun their usual unorganized investigation, they seemed more concerned with controlling the crowd than to find out what happened.

Abrar, Shahid, and Waleed stood together, clutching onto one another for support. As they peered through tear-filled eyes, questions swirled in their minds. How had this happened?

Inspector Abdul Rashid arrived at the grim crime scene with a worn-out leather jacket slung over his police uniform, his hat pulled low to shield his eyes from the harsh reality that lay ahead. He stepped out of his car, surveying the area with a practiced eye, searching for any signs of disturbance amid the growing crowd that had gathered. Approaching the on-scene officer, inspector Rashid inquired about the details of the gruesome discovery. The officer's face held a mixture of grim determination and sadness as he explained the horrific ordeal that had befallen Burhan. 'He was beaten severely,

Inspector, and then stabbed multiple times in the chest,' the officer reported, his voice carrying the weight of the tragedy.

'But there is no blood around, suggesting that his body was discarded here.'

Burhan's uncle approached Inspector Rashid along with the boys. Their faces were etched with shock and grief, struggling to comprehend the brutality of what had transpired. Rashid met them with a somber expression, understanding the pain they were going through.

The boys, their faces etched with a mixture of sorrow, shock, and disbelief, stood near the covered body of their dear friend Burhan. The once-vibrant spirit was now concealed beneath a black rubbery cloth, a shroud that bore witness to the brutality of his fate. Unable to resist the urge to say a final farewell, they took tentative steps forward, drawn to their friend's resting place by an overpowering sense of grief. But their attempts were halted as Inspector Rashid, his eyes reflecting their pain but his duty unwavering, placed a firm hand on their shoulders.

'I'm sorry,' he said softly, but with an air of authority.

'You can't go any closer. It's not allowed.'

Tears welled up in their eyes as they gazed at the lifeless form of their friend, aching to hold him one last time, to make sense of the senseless violence that had taken him away from them. But the inspector's stern but compassionate gaze reminded them of the stark reality they faced.

With a heavy heart, Inspector Rashid began to ask questions about Burhan—details of his address, information about his parents, and any other relevant information that could aid in the investigation. The boys, although shaken to their core, provided the necessary details, their voices trembling as they spoke of their friend. Finally, Inspector Rashid turned to them and directed them to accompany him to the hospital, where Burhan's lifeless body would be taken for examination and to facilitate the necessary procedures.

Meanwhile, in a distant land, Burhan's father, who had been working in the UAE, received the devastating call. Tears welled up in his eyes as he absorbed the news of his son's tragic demise. He wasted no time, immediately instructing his assistant to book the earliest flight available to return home.

Burhan's father, overcome with grief and struggling to find the words, picked up his phone with trembling hands. He stared at the screen, his heart heavy with the task ahead. He had to inform his ex-wife, mother of Burhan about what had happened. Although after a deep breath to steady his voice, he made the difficult decision to ask his assistant to deliver the devastating news to his ex-wife. 'Please, call her. Tell her what's happened. I…I can't find the strength to do it myself,' he pleased his assistant.

His assistant nodded, recognizing the pain in his boss's eyes, and dialed the number to deliver the news that no parent should ever have to hear. As the call went through, the father turned away, unable to bear the anguish of that moment, knowing that the loss of their son would forever bind them in shared sorrow.

In Kashmir, the tragic news of Burhan's lifeless body discovered near the tranquil riverbank raced through the community like a wildfire. The townsfolk huddled together, their voices barely above a whisper, faces etched with a haunting blend of fear and sorrow. This grim revelation, however, was nothing new in these troubled lands, where the ongoing clashes caused many times army or police murder young men during interrogation or protests and either they become missing, or their bodies are discarded. Far too often, the banks of the river had borne witness to the lifeless forms of young souls.

Among the townsfolk, murmurs of concern and grief grew louder, like a gathering storm. Their hushed conversations hinted at a brewing tempest of emotions, one that threatened to erupt into mass gatherings or even protests.

The police officers on the scene keenly sensed the undercurrent of tension in the crowd. They knew that swift action was imperative to prevent an escalation of emotions. Unlike the meticulous investigations seen in the Western world, this region often saw minimal consideration for preserving forensic evidence and safeguarding the integrity of crime scenes. Thus, as soon as the order came down, the officers moved with practiced efficiency.

With solemn determination, they gently lifted Burhan's lifeless body, its stillness a stark contrast to the world it had recently departed. Carefully, they placed him in the waiting ambulance, its doors closing with a heavy finality. The vehicle rumbled to life, departing for the hospital morgue, carrying with it not just a lifeless body but the weight of a community's collective grief and the unsettling knowledge that such scenes had become tragically routine in their lives.

The boys, together with Burhan's uncle, accompanied the police officers to the hospital. Once they reached the hospital, they were directed to a waiting room tucked away in a quiet corner. The room had dim lighting, which added to the heavy atmosphere of sadness. People spoke in hushed tones, sharing their grief and anxiously awaiting news.

Their main concern was to know when they could see their friend's lifeless body and whether it could be released for burial. Time seemed to pass slowly, and with each passing hour, their anxiety grew. The waiting room itself was far from comforting. The bright fluorescent lights overhead glared relentlessly, casting a harsh and unwelcome brightness. The smell of chemicals in the air, a constant reminder of the hospital's clinical environment, added to their discomfort.

To make matters even more somber, the distant sound of a baby's cries drifted through the hospital corridors. It was a poignant reminder of the cycle of life and death, and it underscored the cruelty and beauty that coexisted in their world. As they sat in that room, they were forced to confront the harsh realities of life, a world that could be both unforgiving and filled with moments of profound emotion.

Inspector Abdul Rashid used this opportunity and began by getting preliminary statements from each of them, his tone gentle yet purposeful. The trio, Abrar, Waleed, and Shahid, sat together on one side of the room, their faces etched with worry, and their eyes bloodshot from crying. They recounted last time they had seen Burhan, their voices trembling with emotion.

'He was supposed to meet us at our examination center,' Shahid said, his voice quivering.

'But he never showed up. It's just not like him.'

Inspector Rashid nodded, taking notes as they spoke. He encouraged them to share any details, no matter how insignificant they might seem.

On the other side of the room, Burhan's uncle, a mix of sorrow and anger in his eyes, spoke next. He explained that they hadn't initially considered Burhan missing because he often stayed with his friends during the exam period.

'We thought he was just with them,' Burhan's uncle said, his voice trembling with regret. 'But when the boys told me that he hadn't showed up for his exam, we grew alarmed. This isn't like him at all.'

Rashid listened attentively, his empathetic gaze never leaving the grieving man. He recognized the guilt and pain that plagued the uncle's heart.

Just as the conversation began to settle, the hospital doors swung open, and Burhan's father arrived. His face was etched with devastation, his eyes swollen from endless tears. Rashid's heart ached for the man who had just received the worst news a parent could imagine. With a heavy heart, Rashid expressed his condolences and introduced himself to Burhan's father. He asked for more information about Burhan's background, schooling, and friends. The father's voice quivered as he shared snippets of his son's life, painting a portrait of a young man full of promise and dreams.

The waiting had been going on for hours and suddenly Burhan's mother arrived at the hospital in a rush, her eyes swollen from incessant tears. She could barely stand on her own, and Burhan's uncle hurried to support her. Her grief was palpable, and as she stepped out of the car, she unleashed a heart-wrenching cry, demanding answers about her son's fate. Amidst the chaotic scene, Burhan's uncle tried to calm her, urging her to return home and rest. But her anguish knew no bounds, and she continued to scream, her voice echoing with pain and frustration. Her outburst sent shivers down the spines of those present, particularly the boys who had known Burhan for so long.

In the midst of this emotional turmoil, Burhan's father walks up to her, his face was a mask of grief and anger. The tension in the air was palpable as he confronted Burhan's mother, his words laced with bitterness.

'Where were you all these years?' he demanded, his voice trembling with anger.

Burhan's mother replied, 'I was preparing a life for him in Europe so that he could get away from this shit, where were you, busy with that white whore?' Her grief-stricken face contorted with a mixture of emotions. Burhan's father was almost ready to reply but he stopped himself, contorting to his own lap. The tears flowed freely, not just from Burhan's family but also from the boys, who struggled to accept the loss of their dear friend.

Their sorrow was compounded when the doctors informed them that they couldn't release the body yet due to an ongoing investigation. The lingering uncertainty added another layer of anguish to their already heavy hearts.

As they left the hospital, they were met with a sea of people protesting the armed forces, demanding justice for Burhan. The atmosphere was charged with anger and sorrow, and the boys couldn't help but be swept up in the collective cry for answers and accountability. As news of Burhan's lifeless body found near the riverbank spread like wildfire through the city, the flames of anger and unrest ignited in the hearts of the people of the Kashmir valley. The tragic circumstances of his death led many to believe that it was the work of the armed forces, adding fuel to the long-standing tensions between the protestors and the authorities.

The town buzzed with whispered conversations, growing louder and more fervent with each passing hour. The rumor mill churned out tales of injustice and oppression, further stoking the flames of dissent. Inflamed by their grief and a sense of collective outrage, the people took to the streets, their voices echoing through the narrow alleys and wide boulevards of the valley.

Two weeks after the agonizing wait, Burhan's body was finally released to his family. The funeral procession was a somber affair, a heart-wrenching culmination of the grief and sorrow that had enveloped the valley. Friends, family, and even strangers came together to bid a final farewell to the young man whose life had been tragically cut short.

As the funeral concluded and the last rites were performed, Burhan's mother, her eyes still swollen from endless tears, made the difficult decision to return to the UK with her new husband. Her departure left a void in the hearts of those who had known her and added another layer of sorrow to the already heavy atmosphere.

A few days later, Burhan's father also departed, leaving the valley that had been their home. His grief had transformed into a quiet, simmering anger. He couldn't stay in a place that had taken his son away from him, and he longed for solitude to process his grief and contemplate the path forward.

However, even as Burhan's parents left, the protests continued to rage on. The initial wave of peaceful demonstrations had evolved into a massive movement, demanding justice not only for Burhan but for all those who had suffered in the valley. The tragedy of Burhan's death had become a symbol of the larger struggle for justice and freedom, resonating with people far beyond the Kashmir valley.

The protest, initially peaceful, soon swelled into a mass gathering, with thousands of individuals joining the call for justice. Banners and placards demanding answers fluttered in the wind, while chants filled the air, demanding an end to the perceived brutality inflicted upon their community. The city was enveloped in a sea of people, their unity and determination resonating in every step.

Amidst this unrest, Inspector Abdul Rashid found himself caught in a maelstrom of conflicting emotions. He was called in by the inspector General and was advised to close the case as fast as possible. The protests had continued to swell, attracting national and international attention. Media outlets from across the country descended upon the valley, capturing images of the unrest and broadcasting them to the world. The story of Burhan's tragic death became a symbol of the larger struggle for justice and freedom, resonating with people far beyond the Kashmir valley.

As the days passed, the protests took a more violent turn. Clashes erupted between the protestors and the armed forces, escalating the tension and leaving the streets littered with chaos and despair. Tear gas filled the air, and the sound of gunshots reverberated through the city, creating a symphony of unrest that echoed into the night. The death toll rose with each passing day, as lives were lost in the clashes between the unarmed protestors and the armed forces. The valley became a one-sided battlefield, with the cries of mourning mothers and grieving families piercing the air. The situation had spiraled into a worst-case scenario, far beyond what anyone had anticipated. The quest for justice had unleashed a storm that threatened to consume everything in its path.

A few days later as the protest continued, a young man is brought to the press and is introduced as the killer of Burhan. This man is in his twenties, with a thin pencil like beard and sunken green eyes, he kept looking down, trying to hide his face in a press conference, inspector Abdul Rashid released information that the death of Burhan was related to a girl in their college and Burhan had tried to speak and befriend her and this enraged the arrested youth and thus he found an opportunity to beat and stab Burhan at the dead of night and dumped his body near the river bank using his car. The Inspector also shared that they found that car and the blood of the victim has been found there as well. The deputy inspector general was also present in the press conference, he looked at Abdul Rashid with deep rooted but well-hidden animosity and addressed the people of Kashmir to stop the protests which have claimed the lives of three young men so far and many have been injured.

Abrar and Shahid were watching this this on TV and couldn't believe it, as Burhan was very shy and would never even try to talk to girl in the college, this was not like Burhan. Although now the case was officially closed and they couldn't do anything about it, even though they wanted closure, they just couldn't believe what they were hearing.

The protests had caused for their college to shut down for a few weeks and after the news, the protests died down slowly, and college's reopened. A few days passed, Abrar, Shahid and Waleed were restless, trying their best to continue with their lives but they knew something was wrong.

After the first day of their college experience, marked by the looming shadow of Burhan's tragic death, Shahid, Abrar and Waleed rendezvoused at their usual spot, the Kastoor penj. The atmosphere was markedly different, shrouded in a palpable sense of sorrow that hung heavy in the air.

Abrar broke the silence, his voice tinged with sorrow. 'I still can't believe he's gone; you know? Burhan was the heart and soul of our group. It feels like a piece of us has been torn away.'

Waleed nodded, his eyes glistening with unshed tears. 'Yeah, it's like a bad dream that won't end. We were supposed to have more adventures together, make more memories.'

Shahid, sighed deeply. 'I miss his infectious laughter, his crazy ideas, even his silly pranks. This place, this group, it just doesn't feel the same without him.'

Abrar added, 'Remember how we used to plan our treks and road trips, and Burhan would be the one leading the charge, organizing everything down to the smallest detail? Now, it's like those plans are frozen in time.'

Shahid's voice trembled as he spoke, 'And that night, when we prepared for our midterms and shared stories and dreams…we never thought it would be the last time we'd see him. It's just so unfair.'

Shahid added, 'But I don't believe what they are saying in the news.'

Abrar couldn't hold back his frustration any longer. 'Me too, I just can't wrap my head around it! Burhan, talking to a girl like that? And for that, someone took his life?' His voice trembled with a mixture of emotions.

Shahid, equally perplexed and grief-stricken, shook his head in agreement. 'Burhan had turned his life around. He quit the drugs, attended all his exams. Something's just not right here. We need to get to the bottom of this.'

Abrar nodded, determination flashing in his eyes. 'I'm with you on that, I knew Burhan was hanging out with those guys who were into selling drugs. One of them, I think his name is Ather, used to be close with him. I'm sure he knows something. Let's talk to him, he may know something.'

Waleed thought for a moment, then nodded in agreement. 'We can talk to him and find out what really happened.'

Determined to find Ather and discover the truth, Shahid, Abrar, and Waleed quietly asked around among their college friends, trying to figure out where Ather might be. They didn't take long to piece together enough information to locate Ather's neighborhood. Once they reached the neighborhood, Shahid parked his motorcycle near a small cafe. After finding out which house Ather lived in, they realized they were standing right next to it. They decided to wait for Ather to come out.

Minutes turned into an hour as they patiently sat there, hoping to catch a glimpse of Ather. The sun went down, and the streets grew darker, but they didn't see Ather anywhere. Their mission remained unresolved, and they were left with more questions than answers. Impatience began to gnaw at Shahid. He couldn't sit idly by any longer. Abrar sensed his restlessness and said, 'Shahid, I know it's frustrating, but we need to be patient. Ather could show up at any moment. Let's not rush this.'

However, Shahid's anxiety got the best of him. He decided to take matters into his own hands. He got up, walked up to Ather's front door, and took a deep breath before knocking firmly.

Moments later, the door creaked open, revealing a middle-aged woman, Ather's mother, her face etched with concern.

She looked at Shahid with curiosity and a touch of apprehension. 'Can I help you?' she inquired; her voice tinged with worry.

Shahid: 'Hi, aunty. We're looking for Ather. Do you know where he is?'

Ather's mother was relieved answered, 'Oh, you must be his friends, even we had been looking for him for days. He's been gone for a while now. We were quite worried, but he called yesterday and said he went to Delhi for some computer related educational course.'

Shahid thinking quickly replied, 'Ah, I see. Could you do us a favor? We only have his old number. Could you share his current number with us? It's important that we get in touch with him.'

Ather's mother kindly replied, 'Sure, come in. Let me get my phone.'

As they noted the phone number, they thanked her and walked to the cafeteria and without a delay dialed the number. After a few rings Ather answered the phone but without saying hello.

Shahid: 'Hey, Ather, it's me, your college mate.'

Ather pausing for a while, 'Oh, OK, yeah…how did you get this number?'

Shahid, 'Listen you must have heard about the death of Burhan. It's been tough on everyone, we wanted to talk about Burhan. Before he was killed, did he seem normal to you?'

Ather (pausing), 'Yeah, why are you asking me? He was just fine. Why? (Abrar, unable to contain himself, takes the phone).'

Abrar: 'No, Ather, we know you had something to do with his death! Tell us the truth! We know you were giving him drugs!'

(Shahid looks at Abrar, angry and worried, thinking Ather will hang up)

Ather pausing again exclaimed, 'Oh, I know you, Burhan used to talk about you all the time. Abrar, Shahid, and I forgot the other guy's name. Doesn't matter…look, just drop this. There are powerful people involved just stay away from this. And…why do think I have moved to Delhi.'

Ather hangs up, and the boys try calling him again, but the number is no longer working.

Shahid looked at Abrar and Waleed and whispered, 'What does he mean by big people?'

This proving to be a dead end, the boys didn't pursue Ather further, but they had a burning desire to know what really happened to their friend. Although as time passed, the importance of uncovering the truth behind Burhan's death began to diminish for Shahid, Waleed, and Abrar. They still cared deeply for their friend, but their familial responsibilities took precedence. Abrar was the first to distance himself from the group as he realized his mother had no one else to rely on.

Waleed, despite his best efforts to make time for the investigation, found it increasingly challenging and gradually withdrew as well. However, Shahid remained determined and continued his solo investigation by reaching out to their college acquaintances in search of answers.

# Chapter 8
# Pursuit of Truth

After several weeks, Shahid called Waleed and Abrar to meet him near Dal Lake at a gas station. Waleed and Abrar agreed as they hadn't heard Shahid being this serious or exited in many months. With an air of excitement, he shared an important discovery he had made. 'I have found something crazy!' Shahid exclaimed.

'There is a secret drug house in the Dalgate area where Burhan used to frequent. One of hippies from our college, who has been there too, he was talking to his friends and I overheard him talking about this place and he said he had seen Burhan there once. He was terrified by what he saw and even witnessed Burhan using drugs. I have the address; do you want to come with me? I'm confident we'll find something crucial.' Shahid was pleading to both, afraid they might say no, but Waleed agreed, I have already taken a day off today from work, Abrar paused for a while but agreed as well.

They all hopped on Shahid's motorcycle and embarked on their journey. The search for the drug house proved to be quite challenging, as it was intentionally hidden in an area which was known for tall and thick trees. Finally, they arrived, deciding to observe from a distance before taking any action.

They noticed cautious individuals entering and exiting the premises, raising their suspicions.

Suddenly, a luxurious car pulled up near the house and a young boy, probably 16 or 17 years old emerged, disappearing inside. Shahid's curiosity intensified when he recognized him as Tahir Dar, the son of Minister Ashraf Dar. Determined to uncover the truth, Shahid decided to enter the house. Abrar and Waleed, concerned for his safety, tried to dissuade him, but Shahid remained steadfast in his quest. Eventually, they reluctantly agreed to support him.

Approaching the door, Shahid's heart raced with a mixture of fear and feigned confidence. He summoned the courage to knock, anxiously awaiting a response. After what seemed like an eternity, a person wearing a beanie cap in the summertime opened the door and inquired, 'Who are you?'

Shahid nervously replied, 'I'm…I'm here with Saaqib. He said I should come.'

The person scrutinized Shahid briefly before allowing him inside. As Shahid took hesitant steps closer, he noticed the pungent Odor that clung to the air, a potent mix of burnt substances and stale smoke. The sound of muffled laughter and whispered conversations drifted from within, carrying an air of desolation and despair. It was a place where broken souls sought refuge, their hopes eroded by the seductive embrace of drugs. The house itself stood as a relic of neglect, its weathered exterior bearing the scars of time and neglect. Once a place that exuded warmth and hospitality, it had now transformed into a den of darkness and addiction. The windows, adorned with broken shutters, hinted at the secrets concealed within, their grimy panes reflecting the haunting stories that unfolded within the house's walls.

Shahid's senses were assaulted by the sight and smell of decay, his heart heavy with both fascination and repulsion. He felt an overwhelming need to understand the forces that drew Burhan into this world, a world where shadows danced, and demons whispered promises of temporary solace. Leading him through the unkempt rooms filled with people lounging on a sofa amidst drugs and cigarette butts, he pointed out Saaqib and said, 'Hey, Saaqib, this guy's here, and like I told you last time, you need to tell us if you are bringing someone.' Shahid was struck with fear and didn't expect this investigation to end this early.

To Shahid's surprise, Saaqib, clearly under the influence, played along and said, 'Oh, my bad, man. Sorry, didn't know you were coming. Have a seat.'

Using this opportunity, Shahid sat with Saaqib, pretending to partake in the activities around him. Meanwhile, Saaqib's attention shifted to rolling a joint, providing Shahid with a chance to investigate further. He discreetly made his way toward a partially open door, hoping to overhear a conversation taking place inside.

Peering into the room, Shahid struggled to catch a glimpse of its occupants. He strained his ears, attempting to decipher bits of the conversation. In a stroke of recognition, he identified the young boy as Tahir Dar, the minister's son. Shahid's curiosity heightened as he listened intently, trying to piece together the fragments of their discussion. Caught in a moment of desperation, Tahir's voice quivered as he uttered, 'You don't understand…my father will kill me.'

Yearning to comprehend the full context of their conversation, Shahid desperately sought a clearer view through the slightly open door, eager to uncover the hidden truths concealed within the room. He was about to leave when he heard the name of Burhan mentioned by the boy.

Startled, as he heard the name Burhan, cautiously making his way towards the door of the room. Shahid's heart pounded with a mix of excitement and fear. Before Shahid could fully process the sight before him, the door suddenly closed, blocking his view of the person. Panic gripped him as he realized that the person wearing the beanie cap, the one who had let him inside, was now approaching him. It seemed that his presence had not gone unnoticed. The beanie guy's suspicious gaze bore into Shahid, and he could sense that he was about to be caught.

Instinct kicked in, and Shahid's survival instinct took over. Without a moment's hesitation, he turned on his heels and sprinted away from the room, desperately seeking an escape route. Adrenaline coursed through his veins as he weaved through the labyrinthine corridors of the drug house, his heart pounding in his chest.

The beanie guy, realizing Shahid's intentions, gave chase, his footsteps echoing behind him. Shahid's mind raced, his thoughts consumed by the fear of capture and the repercussions that awaited him. He had come too far to let everything slip away now. With every ounce of determination, he pushed his body to its limits, navigating the twists and turns of the house, desperately searching for an exit.

As he reached a narrow staircase, Shahid made a split-second decision. He swiftly ascended the steps, his footsteps muffled by the chaos below. Once on the upper floor, he found himself in a dimly lit hallway, lined with doors leading to unknown rooms. With the beanie guy still hot on his trail, Shahid's heart pounded in his ears. Time was running out.

Spotting an open window at the end of the corridor, Shahid seized the opportunity. He sprinted towards it, his breath labored, and leaped out into the night air. The cool breeze hit his face as he landed on the ground below, tumbling momentarily before regaining his footing. Shahid wasted no time and continued his escape, blending into the darkness, his heart still racing with the adrenaline of his narrow getaway.

With a safe distance between him and the drug house, Shahid paused to catch his breath. His mind was reeling, replaying the events that had just unfolded.

Burhan's name, the closing door, the beanie guy closing in on him—it was all overwhelming. However, Shahid couldn't let fear overcome him. He knew he had stumbled upon something significant, something that could potentially unravel the mysteries surrounding Burhan's death.

Gathering his racing thoughts, Shahid knew he couldn't afford to waste another moment. The encounter with the beanie guy had rattled him, but he couldn't let fear consume him. He had to find Waleed and Abrar, share his discoveries, and form a plan of action. With his heart pounding, Shahid sprinted towards his friends, his footsteps echoing in his ears.

Reaching Waleed and Abrar, Shahid quickly filled them in on the events that had transpired. They huddled together, seeking solace and strategizing their next move. Shahid's voice quivered with urgency as he explained the pressing need to confront Tahir Dar, to unravel the truth hidden beneath layers of deception.

The days that followed were a blur of restless anticipation. Limited by their access to the internet and reliant on whispers of information, the boys pieced together fragments of Tahir's life. They discovered that he was a high school student at

Tyndale Biscoe School, perpetually shadowed by a security guard—except when he ventured into drug houses. This revelation ignited a spark of hope within them—a chance to approach Tahir in a setting where they could potentially reach him without his guardian's watchful gaze.

Determined to enter the school unnoticed, the trio faced a new challenge. They needed a way to infiltrate the premises without arousing suspicion. It was then that Waleed, drawing upon his past experiences, suggested a daring plan. Having once worked on sewing uniforms for Tyndale Biscoe School, he knew he could acquire the necessary school uniforms to pass as students. Shaving their faces and disguising themselves as schoolboys, the trio embarked on a mission that would test their mettle and resourcefulness. As they reached the school, hearts pacing as they felt like spies, and they had no idea if they can even find Tahir in this big school with 600 plus students.

To their luck, the security guards didn't even check them and granted them entry to the school and disguised as students, the boys navigated the corridors of Tyndale Biscoe School, their hearts pounding in synchrony. With every step, their determination intensified, fueled by the unwavering desire to uncover the truth. They walked for an hour trying to find Tahir Dar but finally, they spotted him.

Tahir was encircled by his adoring entourage, his mere presence commanded attention, a testament to his father's influence and his own charismatic aura.

The boys took their time, patiently waiting for the opportune moment to approach Tahir alone. Their chance came when he separated from his group, striding confidently towards his next class. Seizing the opportunity, Shahid,

Waleed, and Abrar approached him with purpose, their voices laced with a blend of desperation and conviction.

As Tahir's eyes met theirs, curiosity mingled with a hint of fear danced within his gaze. The boys grabbed his arm and dragged to the corner of the school football field. With Tahir isolated from prying eyes, the boys wasted no time in launching their interrogation. Shahid took the lead, his voice carrying a mix of determination, 'Tahir, we want a favor from you, please don't be alarmed we just have a few questions for you.'

Tahir felt confused and scared replied, 'What questions? What are you guys doing? Who are you?'

Abrar knew they had limited time, so he decided to cut to chase. 'We know about the drug house, Tahir. We know about your involvement, and we don't care about that right now. What we need to find out is what really happened to Burhan.'

Tahir now trying to free himself and trying to raise his voice to gain attention replied, 'Who is Burhan? I don't know what you guys want.'

Shahid, sharing glances with Abrar and Waleed, shows his phone to Tahir, with a contact number of Tahir's father ready to be dialed, 'Either you tell us what happened to Burhan, or I will share about your drug use to your father, plus I have pictures of you at the drug house at Dal gate.'

Tahir, his composure crumbling, attempted to flee from the relentless barrage of accusations. But Shahid's grip tightened, his resolve unyielding. The mention of contacting Tahir's powerful father halted his escape, freezing him in place.

A mix of desperation and defeat crept into Tahir's voice as he stammered, 'Who are you guys? Are you even students here? I've never seen you before.'

Shahid, undeterred, reassured him, 'Don't worry about that. We're here to find out the truth about Burhan's death. And we know you were at the drug house last Saturday.'

Tahir's resistance faltered, and he reluctantly admitted, 'Yes, I was there, but I had nothing to do with his death.' And didn't they catch his killer?

Shahid angrily replied, 'That's a lie, we don't believe they story they are selling us.'

Shahid pressed on, determination burning in his eyes. 'Who were you talking to about Burhan at the drug house that day? We know you have information,' he prodded, desperation lacing his words.

Tahir, visibly shaken, tried to compose himself. His voice wavered as he confessed, 'Listen…I knew Burhan, we had partied together in that house and even we hung out a couple of times, but after his death, I had stopped going there for a while. I even have stopped using drugs but the people who manage the drugs and that house started to pressure me, demanding money from me. I was just telling them to leave me alone.'

'Who were you talking to in the drug house that day.'

Tahir shivered. 'I can't tell you that.'

'Tell me or I will send this message and the pictures not only to your father, but to the whole world.'

Tahir visibly shaking and breathing heavy blurted. 'It was the inspector – Abdul Rashid, he is the one who runs the Drug house, how do you think that it is still in operation, his men wanted money to keep my secret.'

As he spoke those words, the boys went quiet and before they could probe him more, the conversation ended as a schoolteacher walked up to the boys and demanded them to hurry up to class. The boys couldn't believe it, they asked Tahir to keep this conversation secret and left.

As they were leaving the school, still in their fake uniforms, they were driven to stop at Kastoor Penj, all of them were silent during the ride, contemplating that this was bigger than them and there were too small and insignificant to deal with this, their anxieties had peaked. They sat down and just blankly looked at each other, it was a shocking revelation and the trio found themselves entangled in a web of corruption and deceit. Abdul Rahman, the same police officer investigating Burhan's case, sent chills down their spines. It appeared that the truth they sought was far more complex and dangerous than they could have ever imagined.

Shahid, Waleed, and Abrar knew they couldn't trust the local police with this information, as it seemed that the Inspector himself was involved in the drug trade. Shahid looked at Abrar and Waleed and said, 'Should we just stop? I don't want to get myself and you guys in trouble, we all have many responsibilities on our shoulders.'

Walled looked at him and said, 'My father always said never lie, and never shy away from truth. I want to find out what happened to Burhan.'

Abrar with his head down whispered, 'Talking about fathers, my father has been missing for quite a long time, I know he isn't alive and probably has been killed long time ago but I can never talk about that in front of my mom, coz she still believes he will come back one day. I can't do anything about that, I can't find out what happened to my father, but history cannot repeat itself and I can't stop till I find out what happened to Burhan, he was my brother.'

Shahid smiled and said, 'I have a big family to think about and every atom in my body is telling me to stop and get away from this, but I just don't want to stop, I just can't…Burhan didn't deserve this, and I also will not stop till we find out what happened to Burhan.'

Shahid finally mustered the courage to share a heart-wrenching revelation with Abrar and Waleed. He confided that he had reached out to Burhan's Dad and Mom, hoping that they would return to Kashmir and help uncover the truth behind their son's mysterious death. Shahid's eyes were filled with sadness as he recounted the conversation, he had with them. Burhan's parents had left Kashmir after his death, shattered, and broken by the loss of their beloved son. Burhan's father who had remarried and his mother who was living with her new husband and stepdaughter, trying to escape the painful memories that haunted them in their hometown. In an emotional tone, Shahid recalled how he had tried to convince them and re-open case.

Although Burhan's parents, now burdened with the responsibilities of their new families, were hesitant to reopen old wounds. They feared that seeking justice for Burhan might endanger their newfound stability and put their new families at risk. Abrar and Waleed listened in silence, their hearts heavy with the weight of this revelation. But with pain and determination they started brainstorming how to handle this.

In their unwavering quest for truth and justice, Shahid, Abrar, and Waleed decided that needed expert help. Their target was none other than Faraz Ahmed, an investigative journalist known for his fearless reporting and relentless dedication to exposing corruption. Despite his unconventional appearance, characterized by polo T-shirts tucked into jeans, Faraz had earned a reputation for his unwavering commitment to the truth. His thick village accent often drew ridicule from some quarters, but it never deterred him from asking the questions that others dared not. With a determined stride, he traversed the city streets, a unique figure who couldn't be easily dismissed.

The trio managed to get in touch with Faraz through a phone call, offering him a glimpse into their chilling story. Intrigued by their account, he agreed to meet them at a discreet spot in the city park, aware that the shadows of powerful figures might be lurking nearby, watching their every move. As Shahid, Abrar, and Waleed revealed the shocking details of Inspector Abdul Rahman's involvement and the potential cover-up in Burhan's case, Faraz listened intently. His expressive eyes revealed a mix of concern for the young men's safety and the sparks of curiosity ignited by their story. He understood the risks of challenging influential figures, but he also recognized the importance of exposing corruption that preyed on innocent lives.

Faraz's decision to help didn't come lightly. Pulling out a stick of chewing gum, he chewed thoughtfully, the gears of his mind turning. 'You're just kids,' he sighed, a hint of incredulity in his voice. 'I can't fathom how you got caught up in this mess. But I'll do what I can.'

With his unique and quirky determination of an amateur journalist, Faraz delved into his investigation. He planned to retrace Burhan's steps in the weeks leading up to his disappearance, weaving together a narrative from the fragments of his final days. He spoke to friends, family, and neighbors, hoping to piece together the puzzle that would ultimately reveal the truth. In his pursuit, Faraz stumbled upon a hidden network of informants. These individuals had spent years quietly gathering information about the drug trade, motivated either by personal loss or a deep-rooted desire to shield their community from the scourge of drugs. Their insights provided a deeper understanding of the complex web that Burhan had become entangled in.

Weeks turned into a relentless cycle of investigation, as Faraz followed leads and pursued every thread, his commitment unyielding. However, fate had more in store for Shahid. One night, as he returned from a grocery run, his path intersected with a police car. The suddenness of the encounter sent shockwaves through him, and instinct took over. A heart-pounding chase ensued, as Shahid darted through narrow alleys, desperately evading the pursuing officers. The chase was a tense back-and-forth, with Shahid narrowly escaping capture multiple times. But in a cruel twist, a stumble proved costly, and the officers managed to apprehend him.

Abrar and Waleed had already been captured, and the trio found themselves in the confines of a police car. Their journey ended at the police station, where Inspector Abdul Rahman awaited them. As they were ushered into his office and forced to squat on the floor, the weight of the situation pressed down on them. The inspector's stern gaze locked onto them, his silence speaking volumes. His words sliced through the air, accusing them of infiltrating Tyndale Biscoe School and attempting to meet someone within its walls. Fear coursed through their veins as they stood accused of actions they hadn't committed. The inspector's verdict was swift – they were to spend the night in a lockup. Desperation laced their pleas, but the inspector's anger only intensified.

'Sir, we're just trying to find out what happened to our friend,' Shahid implored, his voice trembling with a mix of fear and determination.

The inspector's response was chillingly accusatory. 'What happened to your friend? He was killed by that drug addict who's already behind bars,' he spat, his tone laced with disdain. He paused, letting his words hang heavy in the air, before advancing closer to the boys.

'Were you involved in his death? Is that why you're concocting this tale to erase your connection to the crime?' The inspector's words struck like venom, leaving the boys stunned by the unexpected twist. A chilling grin crept onto his face as he posed a terrifying hypothetical.

'What if I find evidence that links you to the murder? What then? Your futures will be shattered beyond repair.'

Silence gripped the room, the weight of the inspector's words echoing in the space between them. Inspector Abdul Rahman's final directive was to have the officers escort the boys to the lockup. The message was clear – abandon your pursuit of truth or face dire consequences.

As they were released onto the city streets, the boys wrestled with a maelstrom of emotions. Fear, anger, and frustration surged within them. Their encounter with the inspector had been meant to instill terror, to break their resolve. But instead, it ignited a fire of determination within their hearts. As the night deepened, Shahid, Abrar, and Waleed found themselves in a city shrouded in darkness. The journey ahead was uncertain, fraught with danger and uncertainty. Yet, as they navigated the shadows, their determination to uncover the truth remained unwavering. Against all odds, they stood ready to confront the injustices that sought to shroud their city and, in doing so, to reclaim the justice that had been denied to their dear friend, Burhan.

# Chapter 9
# The Lawman

In the early days of his career, Inspector Abdul Rashid was an idealistic young man with dreams of becoming something important, he was basically a good boy, did his homework, helped around the house, was responsible and listened to his parents. He came from a humble background, where his father, a hardworking laborer, instilled in him the values of honesty and integrity. He grew up in Delhi due to the transfer of his father's work and because of that he spoke Hindi more than his mother tongue (Kashmiri).

As a proud son, Abdul Rashid was determined to uplift his family's living conditions and bring honor to their name. The only problem was that he had anger issues and he usually was successful in controlling the bursts of his destructive anger, there had been times when he lost his anger and many of times where he seriously injured people.

He could have chosen any career but deep down he knew that the police force might be a good outlet of his anger and he could unleash that anger towards the criminals. Fresh out of the training, Abdul Rashid still believed that he could somewhat eradicate crime and protect the innocent. His intentions were noble, and he held onto his ideals fervently.

However, reality soon shattered his optimistic outlook. As a rookie police officer, Abdul Rashid faced the harsh truth of the system's corruption. He witnessed fellow officers indulging in bribery, extortion, and abuse of power. The lack of respect and low pay further fueled his frustration. He felt undervalued and unnoticed, despite his sincere efforts to make a positive impact.

Abdul Rashid's determination to resist corruption was initially strong, but the constant pressure from his peers and superiors took a toll on his resolve. He began to question whether sticking to his principles was worth the sacrifices he had to make. With financial difficulties looming over him and a family to support, he couldn't help but feel tempted by the allure of easy money.

Inspector Abdul Rashid's descent into darkness started with a tragic incident that took place during a clash with an ongoing protest. His close friend and fellow police officer, Inspector Aamir, was killed during the unrest, leading to a profound transformation in Abdul Rashid's mindset. The protest had erupted in response to the long-standing tensions between the locals and the Indian authorities. The people of Kashmir, tired of oppression and injustice, had taken to the streets to voice their grievances and demand their right to self-determination. In the midst of the chaos, violence erupted, leading to the loss of many lives, including Inspector Aamir's.

The loss of his friend, a man with whom he had shared years of camaraderie and shared goals to serve the society, shattered Abdul Rashid's soul. Grief consumed him, but instead of seeking solace and understanding, he directed his pain towards the very people he had once sworn to protect.

Blinded by rage and hatred, Abdul Rashid developed a deep-seated animosity towards the local population. In his eyes, they were the cause of his friend's death, the reason why he had to endure the anguish of losing a loved one. He began to see the protestors not as human beings with valid grievances, but as enemies who needed to be crushed at all costs.

One day, during an undercover operation, he stumbled upon a drug network operating within the city. This operation wasn't big but had been operating for many years unnoticed. Instead of arresting the criminals involved, he saw an opportunity to exploit their illegal activities for his own benefit. He realized that the drug trade was not only lucrative but also offered the power and respect he so desperately desired.

Driven by the desire for financial stability and status, Abdul Rashid made a fateful decision that would change the course of his life forever. He started by discreetly aligning himself with some corrupt officers who were already involved in the drug trade. He provided them with information and turned a blind eye to their illegal activities, receiving his share of the profits in return.

As time passed, Abdul Rashid became entangled in the web of corruption he had once despised. He felt a strange mix of guilt and power, justifying his actions by convincing himself that he was doing all of this for his family. The money he earned allowed his loved ones to lead a comfortable life, and he convinced himself that it was a necessary sacrifice.

Soon, the once-idealistic young inspector transformed into a shrewd and ruthless drug kingpin. He learned the ins and outs of the drug trade and expanded his network with an iron fist. Some of his fellow officers who had once been his mentors or colleagues became his rivals, and he didn't hesitate to take over their networks by force, resorting to threats and violence when necessary. As Abdul Rashid's empire grew, so did his thirst for power and influence. He manipulated politicians, businessmen, and even more officers within the police force to protect his illicit operations. The more he gained, the more he craved, becoming increasingly ruthless and disconnected from the man he used to be.

Behind the façade of a respected police inspector, Abdul Rashid operated with impunity. He reveled in the fear he instilled in others, and the respect he had once yearned for was now demanded through fear and coercion.

Deep down, Abdul Rashid was still haunted by the dreams he had as a young, determined police officer. He knew he had strayed far from the path of righteousness, and guilt gnawed at his conscience. But it was too late to turn back now, he believed. The web he had woven around himself was too tight to escape.

Amidst the chaos and darkness of Inspector Abdul Rashid's life, there was a brief flicker of hope when he got married. In his younger days, before he became entangled in the drug trade, he had met and fallen in love with a kind and gentle woman named Ayesha. At the time, he still aspired of being a respected police officer and a proud son.

Ayesha was the daughter of a local schoolteacher, and her gentle demeanor and caring nature had captured Abdul Rashid's heart. They were wed in a simple ceremony, and for a brief period, it seemed like the darkness that surrounded him was fading away.

For a while, Abdul Rashid tried to keep his double life hidden from Ayesha. He shielded her from the truth of his involvement in the drug trade, pretending to be the honorable police officer she believed him to be. But as the drug empire expanded, it became increasingly difficult to keep his two worlds apart. Ayesha noticed changes in her husband's behavior—long hours at work, mood swings, and the increasing distance between them. She became suspicious of the secrets he was hiding. Her intuition told her that something was deeply wrong.

But again, the truth was lowly uncovered to the wife, and she has slowly realized that the man she had married was leading a double life, and the darkness she had sensed was real. Feeling betrayed and fearful for her own safety and that of their young child, Ayesha confronted Abdul Rashid. The confrontation turned into a heated argument, with emotions running high on both sides. Ayesha demanded that he leave the drug trade, begging him to return to the man she had once known.

But Abdul Rashid's heart had grown too hardened, and the allure of wealth and power was too strong. In the end, Ayesha made a heart-wrenching decision for the safety of herself and their child. She chose to leave Abdul Rashid, taking their young baby with her. She could not bear to watch her husband spiral deeper into darkness, and she knew that staying with him would only put their lives at risk.

Abdul Rashid's heart shattered as he watched his wife and child walk away from him. In that moment, he felt an overwhelming sense of loss. But the darkness within him was too consuming to allow for redemption. He buried himself deeper in the drug trade, using it to numb the pain of his shattered life. He had lost his morality, his family, and his soul to the corrupt world he had willingly embraced.

In the cold and lonely nights that followed, Abdul Rashid would sometimes catch glimpses of what his life could have been—a life of love, respect, and honor. But those visions were fleeting, drowned out by the darkness that had consumed him.

And so, Inspector Abdul Rashid continued his treacherous path, haunted by the memories of the life he had lost and the choices he had made. His heart had turned to stone, and the faint glimmer of hope that once existed had been extinguished forever. As Inspector Abdul Rashid's involvement in the drug trade deepened, he devised a sinister plan to expand his empire and ensure a steady stream of customers for his drug house. He knew that to maintain control, he needed to keep his clients dependent on drugs, hooked to a life of addiction that would keep them coming back for more.

The drug house was established in a discreet location, hidden from the prying eyes of the authorities and the general public. It became a safe haven for both elite and regular drug users who sought refuge from their troubles and the harsh realities of life. To ensure a constant influx of customers, Abdul Rashid used a multi-pronged approach. He targeted vulnerable individuals, those struggling with personal issues, financial troubles, or emotional trauma. He exploited their weaknesses and offered drugs as an escape from their pain, creating a sense of dependency on him and his network.

Inspector Abdul Rashid's drug operation was extensive and well-organized. He had a network of trusted henchmen and informants under his payroll, spanning across the city and even reaching other parts of North India. These were people who owed him favors, had criminal records, or were lured by the promise of easy money.

At the center of his operation was the drug house, a secret location where elite and regular drug users would find refuge. The drug house was a den of addiction, carefully designed to keep its customers dependent on the drugs supplied by the Inspector's network. He had a team of drug dealers who worked within the house, providing a steady flow of narcotics to the clientele.

The Inspector ensured that the drugs were moved discreetly through the city using various means. Some of his henchmen posed as regular civilians, blending into the crowd as they distributed the illegal substances. Others would transport the drugs using hidden compartments in vehicles to avoid detection during regular checks.

With time, Inspector Rashid's operation expanded beyond the city limits. He established contacts in other parts of North India, where he would supply them with Kashmiri charas, a highly sought-after variety of cannabis that grew in the Kashmir region. This connection not only boosted his profits but also earned him a reputation among drug lords in different states.

The city, once held captive by fear and addiction, was now rallying behind the truth-seekers, demanding justice and a clean-up of its corrupt system. The fate of Inspector Rashid and the city itself rested on the outcome of this battle between darkness and light, a battle that would determine the future of an entire generation.

Using his position as a police officer, Abdul Rashid gathered intelligence on potential new customers. He kept tabs on individuals with a history of drug use or those who showed signs of vulnerability. He leveraged his connections in the force to protect those within his network from being apprehended, ensuring that they remained loyal to him. Once someone became a regular at the drug house, Abdul Rashid ensured they were exposed to drugs of increasing potency. He knew that the higher the stakes, the more difficult it would be for them to break free from the clutches of addiction. He exploited their weakness and vulnerability, trapping them in a cycle of dependence.

Moreover, he made sure his drug house provided more than just drugs. He created a sense of community, a place where users felt understood and accepted. This psychological manipulation fostered a false sense of belonging and camaraderie, making it harder for them to walk away. Abdul Rashid also used the tactic of debt bondage. He would extend credit to users who couldn't afford the drugs, creating a sense of indebtedness that kept them loyal to him. As they spiraled deeper into addiction, their debts grew, further chaining them to the drug house.

The right-hand henchman of Inspector Abdul Rashid was a man named Rafiq Malik. He was a cunning and ruthless individual who had been by the Inspector's side since the early days of his criminal activities. Rafiq was fiercely loyal and had earned the Inspector's trust with his unwavering dedication and efficiency in handling the darker aspects of the drug operation. He didn't look local, he was darker in skin tone with a long Mustache and beard and spoke with a Punjabi accent. Rafiq was not only responsible for managing the day-to-day operations of the drug house but also played a crucial role in overseeing the distribution and transportation of narcotics throughout the city. He had a network of trusted dealers and runners who reported directly to him, ensuring that the drug supply chain remained smooth and undetected by law enforcement.

With a sharp mind and an ability to navigate through the city's criminal underbelly, Rafiq was skilled at avoiding suspicion and keeping the drug operation under wraps. He was well-versed in the art of bribery, intimidation, and manipulation, using these tools to silence potential threats and turn anyone who posed a risk to the Inspector's empire. Rafiq's imposing presence and fierce reputation made him a formidable force within the criminal circles of the city. He was known for his short temper and swift action against anyone who dared to cross the Inspector or disrupt their drug business. His demeanor sent shivers down the spines of both rivals and subordinates alike.

# Chapter 10
# The Investigation

Faraz arrived at the Islamia College on a crisp, sunny morning. It was a bustling place, with students in various stages of hustle and bustle, a cacophony of youthful energy permeating the air. The boys, Abrar, Waleed, and Shahid, stood on the college steps observing the scene, wearing expressions that hovered between intrigue and skepticism. Faraz, in his mid-30s with a slightly disheveled appearance, seemed out of place among the vibrant crowd of students. He wore a worn-out leather jacket, jeans that had seen better days, and a pair of battered sneakers. His salt-and-pepper hair was hidden under a cap pulled low, attempting to blend in with the youth he was about to engage with.

As he wandered through the campus, a hint of determination in his eyes, the students couldn't help but notice the mismatch. Their whispers echoed in the hallways. 'Who's that guy? Is he lost? Maybe he's a new professor?' Despite their curiosity, they maintained a respectful distance from this stranger who had suddenly appeared.

Abrar, Waleed, and Shahid, who had been discreetly observing Faraz, couldn't help but feel a mixture of amusement and concern. They respected his resolve but couldn't help but wonder if he was in over his head. Faraz's method was unorthodox. He struck up conversations with students in the courtyard, at the canteen, and even in the library. His questions were casual, his demeanor friendly, but his inquiries were astute. He probed for information about any unusual activities, mysterious transactions, or suspicious individuals lurking around the college. Despite their initial reservations, Abrar, Waleed, and Shahid couldn't help but respect Faraz's determination.

The boys had a chance to talk privately with Faraz. He listened carefully as they told him about their frightening encounter with Inspector Abdul Rashid at the police station. Faraz could tell that, despite their attempts to appear brave, the boys were actually very scared. Unlike his usual journalist self, Faraz couldn't help but believe them. He comforted the boys and promised to handle the investigation. He encouraged them to focus on their studies while he looked into the matter further. This assurance from Faraz gave the boys hope during a difficult time.

His odd presence aside, it was becoming evident that he was serious about his investigation. He was consistent, he kept coming to the college every day, with different quirky outfits. With some students he played cricket, with some he was delving in religious discussions and the boys were just observing him while going in and out of the classes. The boys watched as their fellow students cautiously responded, sharing stories of hushed deals, unusual comings and goings, and a pervasive sense of unease. Faraz's persistence began to yield results, as bits and pieces of information were woven into a complex tapestry of the college's hidden underbelly.

As days turned into weeks, Faraz uncovered a name – Razak. This discovery sent him on a quest to uncover the enigmatic figure's secrets and shed light on the college's hidden underbelly. Faraz had taken time to follow this man and found out surprising things about him. This enigmatic figure, who resided in the DalGate area of the city and led a seemingly ordinary life with a wife and children, was the linchpin of the entire operation. On the surface, Razak appeared to be a family man, earning a living by driving a small pickup truck. He looked innocent and harmless with a wide smile persistent on his face.

But beneath the façade of domesticity lay a different reality. Razak was the main supplier of hashish and heroin, responsible for trafficking kilos of drugs into the city. His dealings were direct with Rafiq, and he was his prime mule. His web of connections reached both common dealers and high-profile players in the illicit drug trade. His insatiable greed led him to not only sell in bulk but also directly to regular clients.

Faraz knew that unravelling Razak's operation was the key to dismantling the entire network. With the boys by his side, he embarked on a mission to expose the truth and bring the elusive supplier to justice. Their pursuit had taken an even more perilous turn, but they were determined to see it through, no matter the risks.

One crisp morning, they decided to tail Razak, hoping to unveil the source of the drugs that flowed through his hands. As they sat in faraz's 1999 Maruti Suzuki 800 owned, their unassuming presence, a determined journalist and three vigilant students, blended into the bustling streets of Srinagar as they followed their target discreetly.

Razak's movements were deliberate and calculated. He navigated the city's labyrinthine alleyways with ease, a man on a mission. After hours of trailing Razak, their journey took an unexpected turn. Razak, driving his inconspicuous pickup truck, began a journey that led them away from the city, towards the majestic landscapes of Sonmarg. The winding roads of Sonmarg led them to a place that was far removed from the tourist brochures. Deep within the picturesque valley, they discovered a community of horse owners who had been living on the fringes of society. These horse owners, struggling to make ends meet, were at the center of Razak's operation.

It was here that the truth began to emerge. Razak, with a cunning business acumen, had struck a sinister deal with these horse owners. He would purchase the drugs, mainly hashish, from them at a mere fraction of the street price, exploiting their desperation for financial gain. This unholy alliance allowed him to acquire the drugs at an astonishingly low cost, which he would then distribute to his network, reaping immense profits.

Faraz, along with Abrar, Waleed, and Shahid, observed in stunned silence as the illicit transactions unfolded before their eyes. The horse owners, their faces etched with a painful blend of resignation and desperation, traded the forbidden substances for a mere pittance. Razak, his demeanor seemingly friendly, had cunningly befriended and exploited them, ensuring that the drugs were discreetly stashed in his pickup truck beneath the seats. Faraz, with a sense of urgency, discreetly snapped photographs on his phone, meticulously gathering evidence of this sordid exchange.

Their covert pursuit continued as they trailed Razak back towards the city. Along the way, Razak encountered the police not once, but twice. On each occasion, he smoothly handed a substantial stack of cash to the officers through the car window. It became glaringly evident that this drug network was deeply entrenched and intricately organized. Faraz, seizing every opportunity, discreetly captured photographs, revealing the extent of corruption within the system.

The boys were both amazed and appalled by the brazen corruption they witnessed. They felt like insignificant witnesses to a system that thrived on deceit and greed. However, as they observed Faraz's unwavering determination, a glimmer of hope ignited within them. Perhaps, through their collective efforts, they could begin to dismantle this destructive network that was decimating the lives of countless youth.

Their pursuit of Razak finally led them to a small factory near Nowgam area of the city. After parking his vehicle, Razak encountered a tall and intimidating figure. It was clear that Razak held this person in great fear. This imposing individual was none other than Rafiq. Rafiq summoned some men to transport boxes from the factory, handed Razak a thick envelope brimming with cash, and disappeared inside the confines of the factory walls. Faraz, conscious of the need for concrete evidence, diligently continued to capture photographic proof of this clandestine exchange.

After a few days of meticulous surveillance, Faraz came alone convincing the boys to focus on their studies. He had managed to pinpoint the regular rendezvous point at the factory. From his concealed vantage point, he observed the intricate web of the drug distribution network in action. It was a well-oiled machine, orchestrated with chilling precision. Faraz noticed that, after Razak's delivery, several other individuals arrived at the factory, each representing a different facet of this nefarious operation. They were handed their allotted share of drugs, carefully packaged for street-level distribution. It was evident that Razak was just one piece of the puzzle, a cog in the larger machinery.

Rafiq, the mastermind behind this intricate network, had multiple suppliers and mules like Razak at his disposal. Each of them played a specific role in ensuring a steady flow of narcotics into the market. They were given precise targets and territories for distribution, ensuring that the drugs reached every nook and cranny of the city. Faraz's documentation of these events became the foundation of his investigation. But there was no link so far to inspector Abdul Rashid, was he just one of the pawns of Rafiq? Were the boys wrong to think that a full-time employee can manage a drug empire? He planned to visit the factory one last time for further surveillance. This time even he borrowed a proper camera from his other reporter friend, he walked around the factory and found a residential water tanker shaped like a mushroom standing 100 feet tall, he found a way inside and climber the ladder and when reached to the top he could see the inner compound of the factory for the first time. He realized if anyone wasn't looking for drugs, this factory looked like a normal cotton loom processing factory.

He lay on stomach pointing the lens into the factory and after a few moments he noticed a sudden shift in the atmosphere around the factory. Tension hung heavy in the air, and the movements of those involved became more guarded.

It was clear that something significant was about to happen. Intrigued and anxious, Faraz adjusted his camera, preparing for whatever was about to unfold. He remained hidden, his heart pounding in his chest. His years of journalistic instinct had taught him to expect the unexpected, and this moment seemed ripe with the promise of a breakthrough.

Then, like a specter emerging from the shadows, Inspector Abdul Rashid made his entrance. His formidable presence loomed over the scene, sending a shiver down the spine of even the most hardened criminals. Dressed in his official police uniform, he exuded an air of authority that demanded submission.

Faraz's heart raced as he discreetly snapped photographs of this pivotal moment. He knew that capturing Abdul Rashid at the heart of this operation was the key to unraveling the entire network. The inspector's presence in that factory was a damning piece of evidence, one that could potentially expose the corruption and complicity that had allowed this drug empire to thrive.

Abdul Rashid's arrival sent shockwaves through the assembly of drug dealers and distributors. Panic and fear danced in their eyes as they realized that the long arm of the law had finally caught up with them. It was a high-stakes confrontation, with the fate of the investigation hanging in the balance.

Faraz continued to click away, each photograph a snapshot of justice in the making. He knew that these images would be the ammunition needed to bring down not only the drug network but also the corrupt elements within the police force. It was a dangerous game, but one that Faraz was determined to play to its conclusion.

# Chapter 11
# The Fracture

Faraz sat in front of his computer, his fingers hovering over the keyboard, anticipation and anxiety coursing through him. He took a deep breath and began typing the first few lines of the article:

Unveiling the Shadows: A Closer Look at the Underworld of Drug Houses in the Valley.

'In recent months, the valley has been grappling with an escalating drug crisis that has left families shattered and communities in turmoil. It is no secret that these drug houses, disguised as innocent places of refuge, are breeding grounds for addiction and despair. As we peel back the layers of this nefarious network, a startling connection to a tragic incident comes to light.'

Faraz knew he had to tread carefully. The information he possessed was sensitive and could put him and those close to him at risk. He had to release just enough information to raise questions and stir the curiosity of his readers without exposing anyone's identity or endangering lives.

He continued to craft his article, weaving a web of intrigue and hints without divulging explicit details. He described the locations of some drug houses, painting a vivid picture of the shadowy world that operated within the city's underbelly. He referred to rumors of a drug house near the Jhelum riverbank, hinting at a connection to the mysterious circumstances surrounding Burhan's death.

'Could Burhan's tragic fate be linked to these dark alleys of addiction? Could he have stumbled upon something that led to his untimely demise? The questions remain unanswered, and the truth eludes us. He made sure to include the name of Inspector SHO – Abdul Rashid who may be involved in the network.'

The article was a masterful work of ambiguity, a careful dance between fact and insinuation. Faraz wanted to create a ripple of intrigue, prompting the authorities to investigate further while protecting his sources and avoiding direct accusations.

As he hit the "publish" button, Faraz's heart raced with a mix of fear and excitement. He knew that he had taken a bold step, and the consequences of his actions were uncertain. He was acutely aware that powerful forces were at play, and they wouldn't take kindly to someone prying into their illicit affairs.

Soon after the article went live, it began to spread like wildfire on social media. The citizens of the valley, hungry for the truth, shared the piece with fervor.

Rumors and speculations fueled the discussions, and people demanded answers from the authorities.

As the news of Faraz's article reached Inspector Rashid's ears, his face contorted into a mask of anger and frustration. He knew that he had to act quickly to silence any further investigations and maintain his grip over the drug houses. He had once prided himself on his authority and control, found himself at the center of a storm he couldn't control. The article had struck a chord, causing his meticulously constructed drug empire to come under intense scrutiny.

Recognizing the urgency of the situation, he understood that he needed to take immediate action to quash the growing curiosity and suspicion.

As he sat in his office, his phone rang, and it was Arshid, the deputy police commissioner. Abdul Rashid entered his office and closed the door, anticipating that Arshid would not be pleased.

Arshid's voice erupted from the phone, berating him with anger and disbelief, 'What on earth have you done? How does this reporter know so much? You've put us all in jeopardy!'

Abdul Rashid made an effort to soothe Arshid's temper, saying, 'Don't fret, I'll handle this. Besides, haven't I paid you this month? Why are you getting so agitated?'

Arshid remained bewildered, muttering, 'I'll never understand people like you. You have the most aggravating personality. Anyway, listen, there might be an internal investigation. This has gone viral, and everyone is demanding answers.'

Although Abdul Rashid seethed with anger, he begrudgingly acknowledged the severity of the situation. Never had he expected someone to expose his operation to such an extent.

He summoned his loyal henchmen, instructing them to identify the source of the article and deal with the situation discreetly. 'Find out who leaked this information,' he commanded with a steely glint in his eyes.

'And make sure they regret ever crossing me, I am sure those boys have something to do with this. Find them and get them here, this time they aren't going back?'

Unbeknownst to Inspector Rashid, Faraz had meticulously prepared for the potential consequences of his bold actions. He had taken extensive measures to safeguard his identity and protect his sources, acutely aware of the perilous territory he was stepping into. Faraz had no intention of exposing himself to danger; he had arranged to remain hidden in an undisclosed location. He urged the boys to keep a low profile for a few days, cautioning them against seeking refuge with relatives or in any predictable places. The boys understood the gravity of the situation, recognizing that their quest for justice for Burhan required utmost discretion.

Burhan's father, Wajahat, owned an unfinished property on the outskirts of the city. This property would serve as their sanctuary, a place where they could lay low, sheltered from the potential retaliation of Inspector Rashid and his associates. They approached Wajahat, who graciously granted them access to one of his incomplete buildings. It proved to be the ideal hideaway—far removed from prying eyes and nestled within a tranquil neighborhood outside the bustling city.

Under the shroud of night, their emotions ran high as the boys stealthily made their way into the property. The moonlight painted eerie shadows on the half-finished walls as they cautiously ventured inside. Within, the atmosphere bore the unmistakable scent of suspended construction—hints of concrete, dust, and dreams put on indefinite hold. They moved about in silence, their footfalls echoing through the empty chambers. Furniture draped in white sheets awaited a future when it would be unveiled and brought to life. Time seemed to have frozen within these walls, offering a temporary respite from the chaotic storm that had enveloped their lives.

Anxiety gnawed at the boys, and they frequently glanced out of the windows, their eyes scanning the surroundings for any signs of movement. Their provisions were minimal—just a few changes of clothes, some sustenance, and board games to pass the time.

Days turned into nights, and they continued to find refuge within the shelter of Burhan's unfinished home. Their days were consumed by devouring news reports, closely monitoring the aftermath of Faraz's incendiary article. The walls of the house began to press in on them, a constant reminder of their confinement and the looming threat that hung over their heads.

During those tense days, they reminisced about their friend Burhan, whose life had been cut short under mysterious circumstances. His spirit seemed to linger in the very walls of the house, a reminder of why they had embarked on this dangerous journey in the first place. It was in this space that they found the determination to push forward, to face the darkness that had enveloped their lives. And so, as the days turned into weeks, the boys remained hidden in the sanctuary of the unfinished house, plotting their next move, driven by a fierce determination to bring the truth to light and find justice for Burhan.

However, they also knew that Inspector Rashid wouldn't stay silent for long. The corrupt officer would undoubtedly try to harm Faraz or persuade him to stop.

Faraz was prepared for what might come next. He had already made arrangements to stay off the grid for a while, working remotely from undisclosed locations to continue his investigation and keep an eye on the situation in the valley. As the valley buzzed with discussions and debates, Faraz's heart swelled with a sense of purpose. He knew that he had set a chain of events in motion, and the journey had just begun. The shadows were stirring, and the truth was inching closer to the surface. As Faraz's article gained traction and went viral, it sent shockwaves through the region and beyond. The expose not only implicated Inspector Abdul Rashid but also raised suspicions about the involvement of other officers in the police department. The top brass of the police force couldn't ignore the mounting evidence and public outrage any longer. They knew they had to take action. It had become prime news in TV channels across India.

The Police Commissioner himself ordered an internal investigation into the allegations raised in the article. A special task force was formed, comprising officers known for their integrity, to ensure a fair and unbiased inquiry. This decision put Inspector Rashid on edge, as he now faced scrutiny from his own colleagues. Feeling the pressure of the investigation, Inspector Rashid had no choice but to put his drug activities on hold temporarily. He feared that any further action on his part might attract more attention from the authorities and draw suspicion to his involvement in Burhan's death and the drug racket. In a panicked frenzy, Inspector Rashid ordered his henchmen to empty out the drug house, leaving the regular and elite drug users bewildered and desperate for their daily dose. The sudden closure and absence of their addictive refuge caused unrest among the drug users, leading to chaos in the criminal underworld.

To maintain the veil of legality, Inspector Rashid had corrupted certain officials within the police department, who would turn a blind eye to his activities or provide him with information about ongoing investigations. This ensured that his operation remained mostly undisturbed, shielded from prying eyes. But with the recent turn of events, his operation was under severe threat. The article published by Faraz had exposed the drug houses around the city, and the subsequent investigation had Inspector Rashid on edge. He knew that if his dealings outside Kashmir were brought to light, it would be catastrophic for his empire.

The fear of being caught and losing everything he had built over the years gnawed at him day and night. He had to tread carefully now, carefully dismantling his operation bit by bit, ensuring that no evidence was left behind to trace it back to him. It was a race against time, and the once-powerful Inspector was now a desperate man, willing to do whatever it took to protect his empire and himself.

As Inspector Rashid lay low, he felt a sense of betrayal creeping from the shadows of his past. He recalled the days when he joined the police force, full of dreams to serve society and be a proud son. However, the bitter reality of his situation was starkly different. The lack of money, respect, and power had slowly eroded his morals, pushing him toward the path of corruption and crime. He thought about his family, his son was now 14 years old, and he only gets to see his occasionally under the supervision of his mother.

As the sun set over the valley, the echoes of Faraz's article reverberated through the streets, igniting a spark of hope among those who sought justice and exposing the sinister underbelly of the drug houses. Faraz had taken the first step, and the valley held its breath, waiting to see what revelations the shadows would unveil next.

With his initial article, Faraz had only scratched the surface of the drug network operating within the city. He knew that to truly expose the extent of this criminal enterprise, he needed to reveal more details along with the incriminating pictures he had managed to capture. But he also understood the gravity of the situation and the risks involved. Before publishing the next article, Faraz requested the boys to stay hidden for a few more days to ensure their safety.

The publication of Faraz's next article had a seismic impact on the city. As the incriminating details and photographs were unveiled, the public was shocked to learn about the extent of the drug network operating within their midst. For the first time, names and faces of those involved were exposed, sending ripples of fear and outrage through the community.

Abdul Rashid was summoned to the Police Commissioner's office, inside the imposing office of the police commissioner, Inspector Abdul Rashid stood ramrod straight, his weathered face betraying little emotion. The weight of the commissioner's scrutiny bore down upon him. The room was somber, adorned with polished wooden furniture and adorned with the insignia of the law.

Commissioner Khan, a stern man with graying temples and piercing eyes, regarded Abdul Rashid with an unreadable expression.

'Inspector Rashid,' Commissioner Khan began, his voice carrying the weight of authority. 'I have called you here today to discuss a matter of grave importance. These news articles surrounding the drug world and the death of that young boy have cast a shadow on this department, and I need answers.'

Abdul Rashid, with a facade of calm, nodded respectfully. 'I'm at your service, sir. I assure you, I have done everything within my power to uphold the law and maintain the peace.'

Commissioner Khan leaned forward, his gaze unwavering. 'There are allegations, Inspector, that you may have been involved in corrupt practices, that you have ties to the drug trade in this city. I want to hear your side of the story.'

Abdul Rashid's calm exterior began to crack, and his voice quivered with a hint of indignation. 'Sir, I've served in this department for over two decades. My record is unblemished, and I have always strived to protect the citizens of this city. These accusations are baseless.'

The commissioner arched an eyebrow, prompting Abdul Rashid to continue.

'Let me be perfectly clear, sir. I have dedicated my life to law enforcement. I've risked my life on countless occasions, and I've seen colleagues fall in the line of duty. The very idea that I would tarnish the badge I wear with honor is preposterous.'

His voice grew stronger, more impassioned. 'I've spent years tracking down criminals, drug lords, and the scum that prey on the vulnerable. I've put myself in harm's way to protect this city. And now, because of a journalist's articles, my integrity is being questioned?'

Commissioner Khan remained composed, allowing Abdul Rashid to vent his frustrations.

'Sir, I will not stand idly by and let my reputation be destroyed. I will not allow the sacrifices I've made to be in vain. I have dedicated my life to this force, to this city, and to the pursuit of justice.'

His eyes blazed with an intensity that surprised the commissioner. Abdul Rashid continued, his voice taking on a note of anger. 'I demand a thorough investigation into these allegations, so my name can be cleared once and for all. I will cooperate fully because I have nothing to hide.'

Commissioner Khan listened in silence as the monologue reached its crescendo. Abdul Rashid, his fists clenched, concluded, 'I am a reputable police officer, sir, and I intend to prove it.'

For a moment, the room hung heavy with tension. Then, Commissioner Khan leaned back in his chair, his gaze unwavering. 'Very well, Inspector Rashid. Your passion for your duty is evident. We will conduct an investigation into these allegations, and if you are innocent, your name will indeed be cleared. But remember, no one is above the law, no matter their reputation.'

Abdul Rashid nodded, his anger now subsiding, replaced by a steely determination to defend his honor and prove his innocence.

Commissioner Khan's stern expression remained unyielding as he continued. 'However, Inspector Rashid, I must emphasize that due to the gravity of the situation and the widespread attention these allegations have garnered, I have no choice but to suspend you from active duty during the course of this investigation.'

Abdul Rashid's face paled, and he clenched his jaw in frustration. 'Sir, with all due respect, I—'

Commissioner Khan raised a hand, cutting off any protest. 'I understand your concerns, Inspector. But my hands are tied. The public's trust in the department must be upheld. You will be on administrative leave until this matter is resolved.'

With anger raging in his heart, Abdul Rashid nodded, realizing the gravity of the situation. 'I accept your decision, Commissioner. I will cooperate fully during the investigation.'

Commissioner Khan nodded, acknowledging Abdul Rashid's willingness to comply. 'Very well. I have appointed Inspector Insha Khan from Jammu police to oversee this investigation. She comes highly recommended and is known for her impartiality and dedication to the force.'

Abdul Rashid's eyes widened slightly at the mention of Insha Khan's name. He had heard of her reputation and knew that she was a formidable investigator. It was clear that the department was taking these allegations seriously.

Commissioner Khan rose from his seat, signaling the end of their conversation. 'You may go now, Inspector Rashid. Remember, this investigation will be thorough and impartial. It is in the best interest of the department, the city, and your own reputation that the truth comes to light.'

As Abdul Rashid exited the commissioner's office, he couldn't help but feel a sense of unease. The investigation loomed before him, and his suspension weighed heavily on his shoulders. He had to clear his name, no matter the cost, and prove that his dedication to the force was unwavering. Abdul Rashid, who had once wielded immense power, was now facing the consequences of his actions.

The media frenzy that followed the article was unprecedented. News channels, both local and national, picked up the story and ran with it. Reporters dissected the details, experts provided analysis, and talk shows conducted debates on the far-reaching implications of the drug network's exposure. The city was abuzz with discussions about the article, and the public's demand for justice grew louder with each passing day. While the exposure of Abdul Rashid and the drug network was a significant victory, it also brought with it a heightened sense of danger. Those involved in the drug trade, including Rafiq and his associates, were undoubtedly furious. The boys, along with Faraz, had to remain cautious and vigilant, knowing that their identities were not entirely safe.

In the midst of this chaos, one thing was clear: the fight against the drug network had intensified. The article had sparked a public outcry for justice, and the city's law enforcement agencies were under immense pressure to dismantle the criminal enterprise once and for all. Faraz, Abrar, Waleed, and Shahid had played a pivotal role in exposing the truth, but their journey was far from over.

As Inspector Rashid's henchmen scoured the valley in search of Faraz, he was nowhere to be found and on top of that he wanted his men to find Abrar, Waleed and Shahid. Inspector was cunning, he suspected they had something to do with this. The henchmen, well aware of their boss's merciless nature, set out with renewed determination, they tracked down Shahid's family, questioned Abrar's friends, and even surveilled their college. Meanwhile, Faraz kept a constant watch on the situation from a safe distance. He was relieved that the boys were out of immediate danger, but he knew the threat was far from over. He couldn't let his guard down, and neither could they.

Shahid in particular felt torn. He had always been close to his girlfriend Samreen, sharing every joy and sorrow with her. However, he had not yet found the courage to confide in her about the dangerous journey they had embarked upon. He wanted to protect her from the risks and dangers that surrounded them. But as the days passed and the burden grew heavier, he realized that he couldn't keep her in the dark any longer.

One evening, as the sun dipped below the horizon, Shahid found himself standing near the window, staring at the vast expanse of the tees. The river nearby crashed against the rocks, echoing the turmoil in his heart. He pulled out his phone and called Sambreen, feeling a mix of fear and relief as her familiar voice greeted him. He had informed Sambreen that he is staying with is relatives and has gone for a trip with them.

'Hey, Shahid! How's the trip going?' Sambreen asked with enthusiasm.

'It's been good, Sambreen, but there's something I need to talk to you about,' Shahid replied, his voice quivering slightly.

Sensing the seriousness in his tone, Sambreen grew concerned. 'What's wrong, Shahid? You sound troubled. You can tell me anything.'

Shahid took a deep breath and began to share the shocking events that had unfolded back in Kashmir—the death of their friend Burhan, the involvement of Inspector Rashid, and their fight to expose the drug racket. He carefully chose his words, revealing enough to paint a picture without putting her in immediate danger.

As he spoke, Sambreen listened attentively, her heart filled with both worry and admiration for Shahid's bravery. 'Oh my God, Shahid, I can't believe all of this is happening! I had no idea you and your friends were going through something so dangerous. Please be careful,' she pleaded.

'I promise, Sambreen, we are being cautious. That's why I didn't tell you earlier. But I couldn't keep this from you any longer. You deserve to know what's happening,' Shahid assured her. From that moment on, Shahid and Sambreen stayed in constant touch. He kept her updated on their whereabouts, and she became his confidante and a source of strength during their challenging journey.

Back in city, the article released by Faraz had indeed stirred feathers. The expose on the drug houses had ignited public outrage, putting immense pressure on the authorities to take action. Inspector Rashid's desperation grew as his carefully constructed empire began to crumble. As Shahid and his friends continued to stay hidden, they knew they had started a battle that couldn't be easily won. But with the support of each other and their loved ones, and the determination to bring justice to their fallen friend and countless others, they were ready to face whatever came their way. The journey was far from over, but they believed that the truth would prevail in the end. The boys were now getting agitated and tired of staying hidden, they wanted to go back to their homes, but were scared of what was waiting for them.

In the confines of their hidden sanctuary, the boys huddled around a small TV, their hearts heavy with a mix of anxiety and anticipation. The screen flickered to life, and the news anchor's voice resonated through the room.

'In a shocking turn of events, the investigation into the death of Burhan, the young student from the prestigious Islamia College, has taken an unexpected twist. Sources within the police department reveal that new information has come to light, suggesting that Burhan's demise might not be as straightforward as initially thought.'

Shahid's brows furrowed as he exchanged glances with Abrar and Waleed. The room held a tense stillness as the news anchor continued.

'It's believed that Burhan had some financial dealings with one of the individuals recently apprehended in the drug crackdown. Sources suggest that he owed a significant amount of money, and this might have led to a conflict between them. The investigation is still ongoing, and the police are diligently piecing together the puzzle surrounding his tragic death.'

Abrar's jaw clenched as he clenched his fists. 'Unbelievable. They're twisting the truth to protect their own.'

Waleed's voice trembled as he cleared his throat, his face etched with a mix of guilt and sorrow. The room fell silent as the others turned to him, waiting for his words.

'I have something to confess,' Waleed began, his tone heavy. 'There's something I never told you guys about Burhan.'

Shahid and Abrar exchanged puzzled glances, their curiosity piqued. 'What is it, Waleed?' Shahid asked gently.

Waleed took a deep breath, his eyes glistening with emotion. 'A few days before our exams began, Burhan came to see me. He looked very weak and he told me that he was going to quit drugs and he is going to go to a rehab if needed. He had a small bag with him, and the bag was filled with money.'

Abrar's eyebrows shot up in surprise. 'Money? What was he doing with that much money?'

Waleed's gaze dropped to the floor, his voice quivering as he continued, 'You know this universe can play tricks on you, at the same time Burhan was there, I received a phone call from my mom, she was crying as the landlord of my dad's shop was planning to rent it to someone else. We needed 350,000 rupees to save it.'

'Burhan listened to our conversation and saw how tensed I got as this shop was our livelihood and it was my father's legacy in a way and then he asked me to take the bag with money in it, it had around 250,000 in it and said I can at least buy some more time for the shop with it.'

Shahid's eyes widened, a mixture of shock and realization dawning on him. 'Wait, are you saying that Burhan gave you money for that?'

Waleed nodded, his throat tightening with emotion. 'Yes. He gave me 250,000 rupees from that bag and told me to use it to save my father's shop. He didn't want you guys to know, and he made me promise not to tell anyone.'

Abrar's expression softened, his heart aching for his friend's selflessness. 'That's…that's Burhan.'

Waleed's voice trembled as he continued, 'I never got the chance to thank him properly. And now he's gone. I blame myself for not being able to help him like he helped me. Maybe if I had told you guys, you could've found a way to protect him.'

Tears welled up in Shahid's eyes as he reached out to grasp Waleed's shoulder. 'Waleed, this isn't your fault. Burhan's decision was his own, and he did what he believed was right. We can't change what happened.'

Abrar nodded in agreement, his voice firm. 'Those people who hurt Burhan, will be punished I swear.'

The weight of Waleed's confession hung in the air, a reminder of the complexities of their mission. Burhan's act of kindness and his untimely death had further fueled their determination to expose the truth and bring down the corrupt forces that had taken hold of their community. As they clung to the memory of their friend, the boys reaffirmed their commitment to uncovering the layers of deception and unearthing the answers they sought.

# Chapter 12
# The Prey

In the quaint town of Gulmarg, nestled amid the picturesque landscapes of Kashmir, Faraz had taken refuge in a secluded hotel, trying to keep a low profile while continuing his investigative work. He knew that his expose had put him in great danger, but he couldn't back down. Truth had to prevail, no matter the cost.

However, Inspector Rashid's henchmen were relentless in their pursuit. One evening, as the sun dipped below the snow-capped peaks, a henchman named Arif, who had once been a close associate of Faraz, recognized him on the streets of Gulmarg. With a mix of fear and loyalty to the Inspector, he dialed the corrupt officer's number and reported Faraz's location.

Under the midnight sky, a group of menacing figures descended upon the hotel where Faraz was staying. Their footsteps echoed ominously through the empty corridors as they made their way to his room. With cold determination, they knocked on the door, and Faraz's heart sank as he peered through the peephole.

'Open up, Faraz! We know you're in there,' Rafiq growled.

Realizing that escape was not an option, Faraz took a deep breath and unlocked the door. In an instant, the men barged in, surrounding him with menacing glares. Faraz's face was defiant, but his heart raced with fear.

'What do you want?' Faraz demanded, trying to sound strong.

Rafiq took out his gun and pointed at him, he started slapping him, 'You know what we want,' Rafiq sneered.

'You've caused enough trouble for us. We want you to retract that damn article and issue an apology for spreading lies and conspiracies against us.'

'Listen to me, you're making a mistake,' Faraz began, his tone earnest.

'You are all muslims, fear Allah, we are taught that every life is sacred, and that we are accountable for our actions.'

Rafiq, the imposing leader of the group, leaned against a grimy wall. His cold eyes bore into Faraz, an unsettling mix of defiance and disdain. 'Shut the hell up, it doesn't matter,' Rafiq sneered.

'In this world, everyone's out for themselves. You, me, those in power – we're all playing the same game.'

Faraz knew that compliance might be his only way out of this situation. He had no intention of giving up on his mission, but he also understood the dire consequences of defiance. Bruised and battered, he nodded reluctantly.

'OK, what you want? Just don't hurt me,' Faraz negotiated.

The men exchanged glances and then Rafiq chuckled sadistically. 'Oh, we won't harm you. As long as you do as we say, you will be safe.'

Rafiq handed him his laptop and told him that they aren't leaving until he publishes the retraction and a public apology.

As the first rays of dawn cast long shadows across the room, Faraz's trembling fingers tapped out the revised article on his laptop. The weight of guilt and helplessness bore down on him, threatening to crush his spirit. He stared at the screen, haunted by the faces of his one million followers on Twitter, those he had always respected and never wanted to deceive.

The apology was typed out carefully. The link to his withdrawn article on his website, 'Seekers of Truth,' was all set. He had taken back everything he'd said in his last article. He even admitted that some people had tricked him into stirring up trouble in the valley.

Rafiq kept a close eye on Faraz. He was worried Faraz might try something sneaky. Suddenly, Rafiq's phone buzzed. He checked it, then looked at Faraz. After that, he walked over to the window and went back to watching Faraz. Rafiq saw that Faraz's face had changed. He tried to look at Faraz's laptop screen, but he didn't see anything strange. He only saw the letter Faraz was writing. Rafiq didn't know much about computers, so he didn't think much of it and went back to his chair. Faraz remained fixated on the screen, his cursor hovering ominously over the "publish" button, a final, reluctant acceptance of defeat.

Shortly after the article was published, Abdul Rashid's sleek black car pulled into the hotel's parking lot, parking next to a nondescript white pickup truck. He emerged from the vehicle with an air of calculated calmness and made his way to the hotel room. His eyes darted between Faraz, seated before the laptop, and Rafiq, who confirmed that the retraction had been successfully disseminated.

Abdul Rashid, a thin smile playing on his lips, withdrew his phone and verified the retraction. He then gestured for his men to release Faraz's bound feet and took a seat across from him. His gaze bore into Faraz's eyes like a predator toying with its prey.

'You know,' Abdul Rashid began, his voice laced with menace, 'you don't look like a reporter, yet you managed to uncover a great deal about my operation. I must give credit where it's due. You've gained quite the following on social media, but you have also cost me a significant amount of money. You may think you know how much, but I assure you, you don't.'

He turned to Rafiq, a wicked grin curling on his lips. 'Rafiq, how much money have we lost?'

Rafiq, without a change in his expression, replied coldly, 'A substantial amount.'

Abdul Rashid leaned in closer, his eyes locked onto Faraz's. 'Indeed, a substantial amount. Now, I understand you didn't do this alone, did you? Those boys from Islamia College, did they assist you in this?'

Faraz feigned confusion, his heart racing. 'What boys? I don't know any boys.'

Abdul Rashid chuckled darkly. 'Oh, you don't know them? Well, I'll take your word for it. But let me be clear, if I discover that those boys had any involvement in this, I will hunt them down, and their deaths will be merciless.'

Faraz, trembling and traumatized, protested, 'I seriously don't know what you're talking about. I conducted my investigation and found evidence of a drug network. Do you expect that no one would ever uncover your deeds? Every day, young men are dying from overdoses because of the poison you sell, and not a single significant drug bust has occurred.'

A pregnant pause hung in the air as Abdul Rashid regarded Faraz with malicious intent. 'I am letting you go today,' he finally declared, 'but mark my words, if I find out you have written a single word more about our organization or anyone connected to it, I will personally come for you.'

With that chilling ultimatum, Abdul Rashid stood, put on his sunglasses, and exited the room, leaving Faraz gasping for breath. But the room didn't empty as Faraz had expected. One of the men moved to the door, quietly shutting and locking it from the inside. Suddenly, Rafiq loomed behind Faraz, a rope clenched around his throat, and with sheer, brutal strength, lifted him from the chair.

Faraz's panicked screams, choked by the tightening noose, filled the room. His hands flailed wildly, scratching at Rafiq's face and arms in a futile attempt to break free. The other men averted their eyes, unwilling witnesses to this horrifying scene. Rafiq's expression twisted into one of pure malevolence, his eyes bulging and teeth grinding as he continued to apply relentless pressure, determined to extract a final, agonizing act of submission from Faraz.

It takes 6–7 minutes to really kill any person due to strangulation and once Rafiq lets go, a lifeless body of Faraz drops on the floor, the other men throw his body in a carpet, roll him over and lift it to that unmarked pickup truck parked in the hotel parking lot. They drove off deep to the woods and buried his lifeless body in there, with his laptop, phone and his wallet.

In the cold embrace of the night, the boys lay nestled on mattresses spread across the floor of the unfinished house.

Thick blankets were drawn tightly around them, providing a feeble barrier against the biting chill that seeped through the walls. As their breath formed misty clouds in the frigid air, they drifted into the realm of dreams, seeking solace in slumber.

Abrar's sleep was abruptly shattered by the insistent ring of his phone. Blinking away grogginess, he fumbled to answer, his voice laced with sleep, 'Hello? Yes?'

On the other end of the line, a voice oozed like venom, 'Abrar, my boy. Such a pleasure to hear your voice. And your mother, she's a lovely woman, isn't she?'

The drowsiness fled from Abrar's eyes as if a bucket of ice-cold water had been thrown on his face. Suddenly alert, he demanded, 'Who is this? Who the hell is this?'

The voice on the other side chuckled darkly, 'Oh, my dear, no need to get so worked up, you know who this is. I just had a little chat with your dear mother. She was ever so cooperative in giving me your new number.'

Abrar knew this was Abdul Rashid himself, his heart raced, a potent cocktail of anger and fear surging through his veins, 'Listen here, you sick bastard. If you've harmed my mother in any way.'

Abdul Rashid interrupted, its tone chillingly composed, 'Calm down, Abrar. I wouldn't dream of hurting your mother. Now, onto more pressing matters. I have a message for you and your friends. You see, your brave journalist friend, Faraz, well, he's no more. We took care of him. His body now rests in the heart of the forest.'

A strangled gasp escaped Abrar's lips. Faraz, the journalist who had joined their cause, was now a victim of this sinister web they had stumbled upon. 'You're lying,' Abrar managed to choke out.

A cruel chuckle echoed through the line, 'Believe what you will, my boy. But know this – your fate is now intertwined with ours. Come and meet the Inspector. He won't harm you, as long as you behave. We know all about you, and if you even breathe a word to anyone, well, let's just say Faraz's fate will be yours too.' Abrar's heart pounded in his chest like a drumbeat of impending doom.

Desperation colored his voice, 'Please, leave my mother out of this. We won't say anything, just spare her.'

The voice of Abdul Rashid dripped with a twisted amusement, 'Ah, a plea for the heart. Don't worry, we aren't monsters. We're simply the shadows you boys dared to rattle with that article. Keep your lips sealed, and all will be well.' Abrar's hand trembled as he ended the call, his mind racing to process the chilling conversation. He turned to Shahid and Waleed, rousing them from their sleep-induced stupor. In hushed urgency, he recounted the disturbing call that had shattered their fragile peace.

Fear gripped their hearts, and in that dimly lit room, the weight of their situation bore down on them like an unrelenting storm. Abrar reached for his phone, his fingers trembling, and dialed his mother's number. The ringing seemed to stretch into an eternity, until finally, her voice came through the line, a fragile lifeline during their turmoil. Their safety had been compromised, their lives entwined with a malevolent force they barely understood. As they clung to each other, the unfinished house that had once offered them shelter now seemed like a fragile haven against the gathering darkness that threatened to consume them.

The news of Faraz's death hit the boys like a hammer blow. It was a cruel and unexpected twist in their already tumultuous journey. They had grown close to the journalist, trusting him with their lives. Faraz had become more than just an ally; he was a friend and a mentor, guiding them through the treacherous waters of their mission.

Abrar, Waleed, and Shahid sat in the dimly lit living room of the house, their faces etched with grief and disbelief. Tears welled up in Abrar's eyes as he tried to make sense of this. 'No, it can't be true,' he muttered, his voice trembling with a mix of sorrow and anger. Waleed clenched his fists, his knuckles turning white.

Shahid, usually the most composed of the three, stared into the distance, lost in his thoughts. The boys had known the risks of their mission, but they had never imagined losing Faraz. It was a stark reminder of the danger they faced every day. They were now more vulnerable than ever, their protector gone.

Few weeks had passed by and Inspector Abdul Rashid sat alone in his dimly lit living room, a bottle of whiskey on the table beside him. He had always prided himself on being in control, on having power and respect within the police force. But now, that illusion of control was slipping through his fingers like sand, and he was left with nothing but the suffocating fear of exposure.

The article published by Faraz had sent shockwaves through the police department and the city's underworld. Despite the forced retraction, the investigation committee appointed by higher authorities was relentless in their pursuit of the truth. The mounting evidence against the Inspector was undeniable, and he knew that the walls were closing in on him.

The fear of being exposed had transformed him into a broken man, dependent on alcohol to numb the guilt and shame that gnawed at him. He was haunted by the faces of the youths he had killed, the lives he had ruined, and the innocent blood on his hands. As the investigation committee dug deeper, Inspector Rashid knew that he could no longer trust anyone, not even his closest confidants. His henchmen were more loyal to the money and power he provided than to him personally, and he feared that any one of them could betray him to save their own skins.

He looked at the whiskey bottle, contemplating whether to drown his sorrows further or face the truth he had been avoiding. The revelation of his darkest secrets was inevitable, and he knew that he couldn't escape the consequences of his actions. He was a broken man, a shell of his former self, consumed by his own greed and ambition.

As he took another swig of whiskey, he felt the weight of his crimes pressing down on him like a suffocating burden He knew that if he was to be exposed, he wouldn't go down without a fight. The once-determined police officer had now become a cornered animal, dangerous and unpredictable. The investigation he had sparked with his article and a sudden retraction was gaining momentum, and the city was buzzing with rumors about the drug operation and its alleged connections to the police department. Fear and tension gripped the streets as people wondered what revelations were yet to come.

# Chapter 13
# Unshaken

The police officer assigned by the investigating Committee to oversee the internal investigation and the reopening of Burhan's case was IPS officer Inspector Insha Khan. She was a seasoned and incorruptible officer known for her sharp intellect and dedication to upholding justice. Her presence was commanding, not only due to her role but also because of her imposing stature. Insha was a woman of substance, her build slightly on the heavier side, exuding an air of authority that seemed to permeate the room. Her broad shoulders and sturdy frame added to her formidable appearance, while her posture and demeanor showcased years of experience in law enforcement.

With a strong jawline and features that hinted at determination, Insha had a presence that few dared to challenge. Her short-cropped hair was a testament to her practicality and no-nonsense attitude. Dressed in the standard police uniform, she wore it with a certain gravitas, embodying the essence of her position.

Insha Khan's arrival at the location was met with an air of tension, the atmosphere charged with anticipation. Standing before her was the enigmatic figure at the heart of the turmoil

– Inspector Abdul Rashid. As her team positioned themselves, Insha stepped forward with a sense of resolve, her gaze steady on the man before her.

Abdul Rashid, flanked by his associates, projected an image of innocence. He looked at Insha with an almost bewildered expression, as if genuinely surprised by her presence. His lips curved into a disarming smile, his approach designed to downplay any suspicions.

'Why, Officer Khan, what brings you here?' Abdul Rashid's voice was laced with feigned surprise, his eyes locking onto Insha's.

'I must admit, I'm rather intrigued by your sudden interest in this matter.'

Insha met his gaze with a composed look of her own, cautious yet resolute. She recognized the importance of this encounter – a crucial juncture in the unfolding investigation. 'Inspector Rashid,' she addressed him with a respectful nod, her tone measured.

'If I am not wrong you are currently on a forced suspension?'

Abdul Rashid annoyingly answered, 'Yes, I just came to collect a few things from my office, but I want to share with you that I am not involved with this drug business. I have many enemies and they are trying to incriminate me. I am sure police commissioner will understand that soon and let me back from suspension.'

Insha paused and answered, 'Hmmm, and to answer your previous question. I'm here regarding the investigation to uncover any hidden truths that might exist.'

Abdul Rashid's smile grew wider, his demeanor embodying an almost theatrical innocence. 'Truth, you say?'

He appeared to ponder her words with exaggerated thoughtfulness.

'Ah, but truth can be a slippery thing, can't it? Especially in the hands of a determined reporter seeking fame.'

Insha's features remained composed, her eyes conveying a sense of keen observation. She understood the implications of Abdul Rashid's artful words and the attempt to shift the narrative. 'I know reporters in this country can't be trusted but if this reporter made such a big smoke, there should be fire somewhere,' she replied calmly.

'I assure you; my intentions are rooted in the wellbeing of this community.'

Abdul Rashid's façade of innocence wavered slightly, replaced by a flicker of mild frustration. He leaned in, as if eager to explain himself. 'You see, Officer Khan, I'm as eager as you are to uncover the truth. If this reporter's words have led to any misconceptions, I'm more than willing to cooperate in your investigation.'

Insha met his gaze with a measured expression, her tone cautious yet resolute. 'Cooperation is valuable, Inspector, but the truth requires a thorough examination. I won't shy away from uncovering it, no matter where it may lead.'

Abdul Rashid's attempt to cast himself as the innocent party seemed to weaken, replaced by a veneer of defensiveness. He leaned back slightly, his eyes narrowing as he considered her words. 'Of course, Officer Khan. I understand your commitment to uncovering the facts,' he responded, his tone somewhat forced.

Insha's response was a nod of acknowledgment, her eyes unwavering. 'The truth deserves to be heard, and justice demands its due.'

Their interaction bore the undercurrent of a subtle confrontation – a clash of intentions veiled by carefully chosen words. Insha remained steadfast, asserting her determination to unveil the truth no matter how the situation unfolded. As she turned to confer with her team, a renewed sense of purpose kindled within her – a fire that would fuel her pursuit of justice without compromise.

As she delved into the case files and re-examined the evidence presented by Inspector Abdul Rashid, she couldn't help but notice inconsistencies and discrepancies. With every piece of evidence she reviewed, the doubts grew in her mind. There were witness statements that seemed coerced, forensic reports that appeared tampered with, and crucial pieces of evidence that had conveniently gone missing. Insha was certain that something was amiss, and it was evident that Abdul Rashid had tried to cover his tracks. Despite the mounting pressure from higher authorities to close the case quickly, Insha remained steadfast in her commitment to finding the truth. She knew that the lives of innocent people were at stake, and justice demanded a thorough and impartial investigation.

As Insha continued her probe, she faced resistance from some within the police department who were loyal to Abdul Rashid and involved in the drug racket. They tried to intimidate her, warning her of dire consequences if she didn't back off.

But Insha's determination only grew stronger, and she refused to be swayed by their threats. Even the medical report of Burhan wasn't consistent with the report shared by the police department. But her focus had to be drug network and with some quality police work she figured out the possible locations of the drug houses and in the days that followed, a wave of crackdowns swept through the city. Inspector Insha Khan's determination to clean the streets of criminal elements grew stronger. Her efforts bore fruit as she managed to apprehend several of Rafiq's men, dismantling a portion of his illicit network. Insha's unwavering commitment to justice began to garner respect from some corners of the force, while in others, it ruffled feathers and triggered whispers of unrest.

As the web of intrigue continued to tighten, a whisper reached the ears of Inspector Insha Khan. It was a rumor at first, a hushed conversation among officers, and then it slowly rippled through the police station like a shadowy secret. Faraz Ahmed, the journalist who had ignited this firestorm of investigations, had vanished. There were no traces, no clues left behind. He had simply vanished into thin air. Inspector Insha's curiosity was piqued. She had held conversations with Faraz before, his relentless pursuit of truth often unnerving yet intriguing her. Despite his eccentricities, she had found his passion admirable, his intentions pure. Now, faced with his disappearance, a nagging sense of unease settled in her gut.

However, amidst the chaos of her duties, something unexpected happened. Insha's young daughter calls her and asks her to check her emails as her school must have sent her some forms to fill. While checking her personal emails she found an email that had landed in her inbox and she had missed it, it was from Faraz, the missing reporter, it only contained a message of one line:

*Find the boys from Islamia College, they are in danger with an attachment of an image which Faraz hadn't made public yet, a picture of Abdul Rashid handling drugs at the factory along with Rafiq.*

A stark message from the journalist who is missing or dead. Faraz's words spoke directly to Insha's heart, resonating with a plea that couldn't be ignored.

Insha's mind raced as she tried to understand who the boys from Islamia College were. A shiver ran down her spine as the puzzle pieces clicked into place. She had read reports of the friends of Burhan, and she ran to the filing room to get their names, she asked the officers to call them up and find the immediately. The officers came back saying they are nowhere to be found, they visited their home and even the parents had no idea where they were. Some of the officers loyal to Abdul Rashid even remarked, I guess, these boys must have killed that Burhan boy and now are hiding, Insha Khan was more intelligent to take head. She realized that Faraz was captured and could only send this short message even in his dire circumstances and somehow managed to reach out to her. The message was his lifeline, his last hope that the truth would continue to be unveiled.

Torn between her duty as an officer of the law and her growing realization of the depths of corruption that had ensnared her own colleagues, Insha faced a choice. She knew that if she ignored the message, the boys would be lost in the crossfire, victims of a power struggle that had spiraled out of control.

Insha Khan's determination led her to a pivotal knowledge. She knew that the boys from Islamia College could be prime witnesses to a tangled web of corruption and deceit that has been created. Unfortunately, they were nowhere to be found, Insha had a bright moment and decided to seek the aid of Burhan's father. She tracked him down, a sense of urgency propelling her steps. It wasn't just about her duty anymore; it was about protecting the innocent and unearthing the truth. She could sense the echoes of his pain through his words.

The wounds of loss were etched deep within him, and she knew that reopening those wounds might be a painful task. But she also knew that he was their only hope – the bridge that could lead them to the boys who were now hiding from the storm they had inadvertently stirred.

With a calm yet earnest demeanor, Insha explained the gravity of the situation. She painted a picture of the dangerous game that had been set into motion, a game where innocent lives were mere pawns. She implored him to understand that the boys' safety depended on their willingness to cooperate, to stand as witnesses against the very forces that sought to silence them. Burhan's father listened intently, his eyes flickering with a mix of concern and determination. He knew that it was time to step up, to honor his son's memory by standing up for the truth. He picked up the phone and dialed the number he knew by heart – the number of the boys he had come to think of as his own sons.

Meanwhile, hidden away in an unfinished property, Shahid, Abrar, and Waleed were living in a state of perpetual uncertainty. The phone's ring broke through the tense silence of their makeshift hideout. The screen displayed a familiar number – Burhan's father. As Shahid answered the call, his heart raced, unsure of what news awaited them.

The voice on the other end was familiar yet laced with urgency. Burhan's father's words were a lifeline, a beacon of hope cutting through the darkness. Insha Khan was sending someone to pick them up – Burhan's father had convinced them that Insha Khan understood the gravity of the situation, she was willing to put her own career and life on the line to protect them. Relief washed over them, mingled with a newfound trust in the relentless inspector. In that moment, the boys understood that they weren't alone in this fight. They were being offered a lifeline, an opportunity to stand up against the shadows that had haunted their lives.

As they gathered their belongings and prepared to face the uncertain path ahead, Shahid, Abrar, and Waleed knew that their lives were about to change once again. But this time, it was different. This time, they had an ally who believed in the power of truth, an ally who was willing to go to great lengths to ensure justice prevailed. Insha Khan's unwavering dedication had ignited a spark of hope in the midst of chaos, and they were ready to follow that spark, wherever it led. With a firm resolve, she pocketed her phone, the email was etched into her memory. She would find the boys from Islamia College, and together, they would confront the darkness that had consumed their lives. Insha Khan, the relentless inspector, would become a beacon of hope in a world where truth and justice seemed like distant echoes.

Insha Khan's was piecing this together and had a hunch about the danger that Shahid, Abrar, and Waleed were in, and she was determined to do whatever it took to ensure their safety. She sent a trusted police officer to pick them up from their hiding place. As the police car approached the unfinished property where the boys were hiding, a sense of relief and anxiety swept over them. Their hope was palpable as they saw the familiar uniform of a police officer stepping out of the car.

They rushed to greet him, their faces a mix of apprehension and gratitude. The officer nodded at them, a gesture that spoke volumes – they were in good hands.

However, fate had a different plan. Unbeknownst to them, danger was lurking in the shadows. As the police car pulled up to the house, another vehicle – a white pickup truck – followed closely behind. It was the same truck that had been associated with Rafiq, the enigmatic figure at the heart of the unfolding chaos. The sight of these men sent shivers down their spines, casting a cloud of uncertainty over the situation.

Fear tightened its grip around them as realization dawned – this wasn't a rescue; it was a trap. The police officer's loyalty was to someone else, and that someone was undoubtedly linked to the nefarious network they had been trying to expose. With a sinking feeling, they were roughly dragged towards the waiting pickup truck. Their pleas fell on deaf ears as the grip on their arms tightened, and their hopes shattered like fragile glass. The officer's betrayal was a harsh reminder of the complexities they were entangled in. The police car that had once symbolized safety now felt like a prison, carrying them towards a confrontation they had desperately tried to avoid.

As they were forced into the pickup truck, the weight of their vulnerability settled heavily upon them. The world had turned against them, and the very people who were meant to protect and serve had become instruments of their persecution.

The road ahead was uncertain and treacherous, and as the pickup truck merged into traffic, they could only wonder what awaited them at the end of this journey.

# Chapter 14
# The Game

Insha Khan's heart raced as she waited for the call from her officer. The minutes stretched on like hours, and her worry only deepened. When the call finally came, her instincts screamed that something was amiss. The officer's voice sounded strained and hurried as he reported that they had arrived at the location, but the boys were nowhere to be found. It was as if they had vanished into thin air.

A knot of suspicion tightened in Insha's chest. She had trusted this officer, believed in his loyalty, and now his words felt like a betrayal. Could he have been compromised? Was there a hidden agenda at play? These questions swirled in her mind, gnawing at her thoughts and casting doubt on the very foundation of her work.

Without wasting a moment, Insha rushed to the police station, her determination fueling her steps. She knew that the key to unravelling this mystery lay within the walls of the lockup. Her gaze settled on a group of men who had been recently arrested during the crackdown on the drug trade. They sat in a dimly lit, windowless room at the police station, their faces etched with a mix of defiance and fear. Insha

Khan's presence was imposing, her resolve unwavering as she sought answers.

She began the interrogation with a stern tone, 'Listen, we have evidence linking you all to the drug operations. We know you're involved, and we're giving you a chance to cooperate. Tell us everything you know, and we might consider reducing your sentences.'

The room remained silent for a moment; the tension palpable. The individuals exchanged cautious glances, sizing up the determined inspector before them. One of them, a man with a weathered face and hardened eyes, finally spoke, 'You've got nothing on us. We won't say a word.'

Insha Khan's patience wore thin, but she maintained her composure. She knew that breaking these men's silence would be a challenging task. She leaned forward and, in a calm but firm voice, continued, 'You assholes, you may think silence is your best defense, but I assure you, it won't protect you for long.'

Insha began hitting the prison cell bars with her baton to instill fear in them and continued, 'We have a strong case, and we're closing in on your associates. The only way to help yourselves now is to cooperate. Think about your families, your futures.'

Another man, younger but equally resolute, scoffed, 'Our families have survived worse. We're not afraid of your threats.'

Insha Khan's jaw clenched, but she remained resolute. She knew that these men were deeply entrenched in a world of secrecy and fear. Breaking their loyalty to Abdul Rashid wouldn't be easy, but she couldn't afford to give up.

'You are fucked either way, either I put the charges for selling drugs on each one of you or I go easy on you guys, that is, if you help me,' Insha Khan warned, rising from her chair. 'It's your choice for now but trust me if you don't cooperate, I will ensure that you never come out of prison.'

Among them, she spotted a man whose eyes held a mixture of fear and hope and tiny bit of resolve to help, but Insha khan had lost hope of any help from these men, and she leaves feeling distraught.

During all of this, boys were in big trouble. The boys' hearts pounded in their chests as they were driven to an unknown location. Their thoughts raced, trying to make sense of the dire situation they found themselves in. Fear and confusion mingled, creating a toxic cocktail of emotions. The police officer who had arrived to pick them up had betrayed them, and now they were at the mercy of the ruthless forces that had been orchestrating the cover-up.

The white truck came to a halt, and the boys were roughly pulled out and led into a dimly lit building. The air was heavy with tension, and the sounds of their own footsteps echoed through the corridor as they were pushed forward. With each step, their anxiety grew, the weight of the situation bearing down on them like a suffocating cloud.

They were led into a storage room, its walls lined with shelves stacked high with packages. The room reeked of a pungent odor, a sickly-sweet smell that made their stomachs churn. The realization struck them like a blow – they were surrounded by the very drugs they had been investigating, the drugs that had led to Burhan's death and Faraz's murder.

Their captors wasted no time. Harsh blows rained down on them, their bodies absorbing the pain as they were beaten without mercy. The boys fought to stay on their feet, their minds a blur of agony and desperation. The room spun around them, and they struggled to comprehend the nightmare that had become their reality. As the beating continued, the boys' strength began to wane. Bloodied and bruised, they were finally left crumpled on the cold, unforgiving floor. Their tormentors had made their message clear – they were powerless, at the mercy of those who held them captive.

Time passed in a haze, the boys trapped in the suffocating darkness of the storage room. Pain throbbed through their battered bodies, and the sting of their injuries was a constant reminder of the danger they were in. Fear gnawed at them, their minds racing with thoughts of what might come next.

Hours stretched on, the room growing colder as the night deepened. In the midst of their pain and despair, a glimmer of hope emerged. As they huddled together in the dim storage room, they waited, their hearts echoing the same plea – to be rescued from the clutches of darkness and brought back into the light.

The hours stretched into what felt like an eternity. The boys, bruised and broken, huddled in the cold storage room, their minds tormented by fear and uncertainty. The hope that had once burned brightly within them began to flicker, replaced by doubt and despair. As the night wore on, their thoughts turned to Insha Khan, the person they had hoped would be their savior.

Their trust in Insha had been shaken by the events that had unfolded. The police officer's betrayal had cast a shadow of doubt over her, leaving them to believe that she is one of them. They couldn't ignore the possibility that she might have been part of a larger plan to trap them, to ensure their silence once and for all. The realization dawned on them – they were alone, abandoned in a web of treachery. As they huddled in the darkness, the room seemed to close in around them, their breaths shallow and labored. Every creak of the building, every distant sound, sent shivers down their spines. The drugs on the shelves around them seemed to mock their predicament, a cruel reminder of the danger they were immersed in.

The flicker of hope that had sustained them began to fade, replaced by a growing sense of inevitability. They exchanged worried glances, unspoken questions passing between them. Would they ever see the light of day again? Had their pursuit of truth led them to this grim end? The weight of their situation bore down on them, an unbearable burden of uncertainty. As the night wore on, exhaustion and pain gnawed at their bodies, yet their minds remained alert, consumed by the dire circumstances they faced. They replayed every interaction, every decision, searching for clues they might have missed, signs that could have warned them. Doubt had become a suffocating presence, poisoning their thoughts and sowing seeds of mistrust.

As the night drew on and the darkness deepened, their strength waned. The walls of the storage room seemed to close in, and the weight of their injuries grew heavier. Each passing moment pushed them closer to the edge of surrender, to the belief that their struggle was in vain. In the depths of the night, a cold realization settled over them – they were truly on their own. The flicker of hope had dimmed, leaving behind a chilling void. As they clung to each other, seeking solace in their shared fear, the prospect of their impending fate loomed large.

Two agonizing days had passed since the boys were captured by Abdul Rashid's men. The days had stretched into an agonizing wait for the families of Abrar and Shahid. The worried mothers, in particular, could no longer bear the silence and uncertainty surrounding their children's whereabouts. It had been days since they last heard from them, and the anxiety had reached a breaking point.

With heavy hearts and eyes filled with worry, Abrar's mother and Shahid's family gathered their courage and decided to visit the police station. They had heard rumors about the recent activities involving Inspector Insha Khan and her relentless pursuit of justice. With trembling hands, they hoped that she might have some information about their missing sons.

As they entered the police station, their faces etched with concern, they were directed to Inspector Insha Khan's office. She sat behind her desk, poring over files and evidence, her dedication to the case unwavering. When the mothers and Shahid's family entered her office, she looked up, her eyes mirroring their shared concern.

Abrar's mother, her voice trembling, implored, 'Please, Inspector madam, we haven't heard from our sons in days. We don't know where they are, and we're terrified. Can you help us find them?'

Shahid's family nodded in agreement, their eyes filled with tears and apprehension. Insha Khan's heart went out to these distraught families. She knew that the missing boys were a crucial part of the ongoing investigation, and their safety was of paramount importance.

Insha Khan assured them as gently as she could, 'I understand your concerns, and I promise you that we are doing everything we can to locate your sons. They are linked to a critical case we're investigating. Please have faith in our efforts, and I'll keep you updated on any developments.'

The families, while still deeply worried, found some solace in Insha Khan's words. They knew that she was their best hope of reuniting with their sons and finding answers. With heavy hearts, they left the police station, their prayers and hopes now firmly placed in the hands of Inspector Insha Khan and the relentless pursuit of justice.

Insha Khan, fueled by a relentless determination to find them and dismantle the criminal network, had been working tirelessly. Her every waking moment was dedicated to this mission, and sleep had become an elusive luxury.

The police station was a hub of activity, with officers and investigators pouring over every lead and piece of evidence. Insha Khan herself had barely left her office, surrounded by case files, and a growing stack of empty cups of chai. Her eyes bore the heavy burden of sleepless nights, but her spirit remained unbroken. In the government issued apartments she took time to shower and call her family back in Jammu before heading back. She couldn't get the images of the parents of the boys out of her mind and decides to interrogate the man she had noticed earlier in the prison cell.

Rizwan, a worn and anxious figure, was dragged in an austere interrogation room, the air was thick with tension. A lone overhead light cast stark shadows, emphasizing the grim atmosphere. Inspector Insha Khan was seated across, and his hands trembled slightly, his eyes darting around as if searching for an escape.

Insha's approach was determined and no-nonsense. She locked eyes with the man and demanded answers. Her voice was unwavering, her authority unchallenged. 'Tell me, she demanded, 'where are your hideouts in the valley?'

'Rizwan, is your name right, looking into a paper,' Insha's voice was a steel thread, cutting through the silence like a blade. 'You're in a tight spot here, and the evidence is stacking up against you. We know you've been in pocket of some corrupt police officers for years, pulling strings for them.'

Rizwan's gaze fell to his fidgeting hands, beads of sweat forming on his forehead. His fear was palpable, a suffocating weight that seemed to press down on him.

'You think you're just a pawn in this game, don't you?' Insha's tone was relentless, her eyes narrowing as she leaned forward. 'But I've seen this before, Rizwan. Men like you start small, doing the dirty work, thinking you're building something. And then, before you know it, you're in so deep that there's no way out.'

Rizwan's gaze met Insha's, a mixture of apprehension and desperation. 'I swear, I didn't sign up for this thinking it would lead here,' he stammered, his voice cracking.

But Abdul Rashid, he's not a man you cross. He holds power over everything – our lives, our families.'

Insha's voice remained unwavering; her eyes locked onto Rizwan's. 'We've connected you to the operations, Rizwan. The drug trafficking, the violence – it's all on your hands, and trust me if I don't find those boys, I will personally make sure you never see the daylight.'

Rizwan's breath hitched as he finally met Insha's gaze. There was something in her eyes, a blend of determination and understanding that unnerved him. 'What do you want from me?' he whispered, his voice a fragile thread.

Insha leaned in closer, her voice lowering to a dangerous whisper. 'The truth. About Abdul Rashid's involvement and what do you know about the boys from Islamia College.'

Rizwan hesitated, his mind warring with his fear. But there was something about Insha's presence that compelled him to speak, to unburden the truth he had been hiding.

Rizwan nodded, his gaze falling to his trembling hands. 'OK, I will tell you everything just promise me I will be let free, although I don't know anything about those boys, all I know is that, our Boss, Rafiq has been trying to find them for some time.'

A heavy silence settled in the room, broken only by the sound of Rizwan's ragged breaths. Insha sat back, absorbing the weight of Rizwan's confession. 'You've been complicit in crimes, Rizwan. But now, you have a chance to make amends, I can't promise you immediate freedom but I can help you to get out of here faster.'

Rizwan's eyes glistened with unshed tears; his vulnerability laid bare. 'What do you want me to do?'

Insha's gaze softened slightly; her tone tinged with empathy. 'Cooperate. Testify against Abdul Rashid. Help us dismantle this network you've been entangled in.'

As the words hung in the air, Rizwan's resolve seemed to solidify. He met Insha's gaze with a newfound determination.

Later that day, Insha Khan stood outside the office of the police commissioner. Her heart raced, knowing that the revelations she held could shake the foundation of the department. But she was resolute – the truth needed to be unveiled, and justice demanded to be served.

Insha's knuckles rapped against the commissioner's office door, the sound echoing down the hallway. Moments later, the door swung open, revealing

Commissioner Qureshi, a stern and imposing figure known for his no-nonsense approach.

'Detective Khan,' he greeted with a nod. 'What brings you here?'

Insha wasted no time, her gaze steady as she spoke. 'Commissioner, I've been investigating the drug trade and the murder of the young boy. I've uncovered evidence that points directly to Inspector Abdul Rashid's involvement, at least towards the drug trade and recently I found out about three boys who could be crucial witnesses, although I have a reason to believe that Abdul Rashid's men got to them before me.'

Commissioner Qureshi's brows furrowed, his eyes narrowing as he studied Insha's determined expression. 'Abdul Rashid? Are you sure about this?'

Insha nodded; her voice unwavering. 'Yes, sir. Besides I have testimony from an insider who was involved in the operations. He's willing to testify against Rashid. Plus, I have received an email from the journalist Faraz, he shared this picture with me.'

The commissioner's jaw clenched as he looked at the picture, his grip on the edge of his desk tightening. 'This is a serious allegation, Khan. Abdul Rashid is a respected officer.'

Insha's gaze didn't waver, her resolve unshaken. 'Respected on the surface, perhaps. But beneath that facade, there's a network of corruption and crime that needs to be exposed.'

The commissioner leaned back in his chair, sighing heavily. 'And what do you propose, Detective?'

'I propose that we move forward with an arrest warrant for Abdul Rashid,' Insha replied firmly. 'He is already suspended until the investigation and we have enough evidence to at least bring him in for questioning, I know we either do it publicly and tarnish our own police force's name or and I am sure you will agree, we do it quietly and put him in custody till the case is filed at the magistrate.'

Commissioner Qureshi's gaze met Insha's, a complex mixture of skepticism and consideration. After a tense moment, he finally spoke. 'All right, Khan. I'll approve the warrant. I can sure you understand the politics behind this, but remember, this is a delicate situation. We need concrete evidence before we tarnish an officer's reputation, and you will need to do this very quietly, no press or any rumors going around.'

Insha nodded, gratitude evident in her eyes. 'Thank you, sir. I'll ensure that the investigation proceeds with the utmost professionalism.'

As she left the commissioner's office, Insha's mind raced with a whirlwind of thoughts and emotions. Although as she and her team reached the residence of Abdul Rashid, he was long gone. Insha looked at her team suspiciously and kicked the door in disgust.

In the confines of the storage room, the boys strained their ears, their battered bodies frozen with dread as they listened to the murmur of voices outside. The voices grew clearer, and their blood ran cold as they recognized the unmistakable tone of Abdul Rashid. Their hearts pounded in their chests as they realized that the very man, they had been trying to expose was now just a few feet away from them.

Their injuries forgotten, the boys pressed themselves against the cold walls, desperate to catch every word of the conversation that unfolded just beyond their prison.

'Rafiq, you need to understand the gravity of the situation. Insha Khan is on to us. She's got a damn warrant against me, against all of us.'

Rafiq's reply was a mix of resignation and frustration. 'I know, Sirji. But how did she find out? How did she get that warrant?'

Abdul Rashid's voice dripped with irritation. 'I don't know yet, Rafiq. Maybe one of our men who was captured must have broken, but what matters now is that we stay ahead of her. We can't afford any slip-ups. If she catches us, everything will crumble.'

Rafiq's tone was edged with concern. 'And what about those boys we've got locked up? What are we gonna do with them?'

Abdul Rashid's words were laced with a dangerous edge. 'Those boys are trouble, Rafiq. They've poked their noses too deep. We can't let them leave here alive. We can't risk them exposing us.'

There was a heavy silence, broken only by the muffled sounds of shuffling and distant whispers from the storage room where the boys were held captive.

Rafiq's voice held a note of unease. 'So, what's the plan, Inspector?'

Abdul Rashid's response was swift and cold. 'We deal with them tonight. We take them out of the equation. I don't care how you do it, just make sure it's done before Insha Khan gets too close.'

Rafiq's voice lowered further, laden with a sense of grim determination. 'Consider it done, Inspector. Those boys won't be a problem anymore.'

Outside the storage room, the boys exchanged wide-eyed glances. The truth of their dire situation hung heavy in the air as they listened to the sinister conversation. It was clear that their lives were hanging by a thread, that Abdul Rashid's desperation had pushed him to take extreme measures.

Their hearts pounded in their chests, a mixture of fear and anger fueling their resolve. They were running out of time, but they were not defeated. The conversation they had overheard only steeled their determination to escape, to bring the truth to light, and to outwit the very men who sought to silence them.

As they clung to each other and to the faint glimmer of hope, the boys knew that the coming hours would test their courage and resourcefulness like never before. But they were not alone – they had each other, and they had the memory of their friend Burhan urging them forward. With a silent promise to stand strong and fight back, they braced themselves for the challenges that lay ahead, ready to confront the darkness head-on in their pursuit of justice.

As the conversation outside continued, the boys exchanged worried glances. Their survival instincts kicked in, and they knew that they had to find a way out, and fast. The realization that Abdul Rashid was standing just a few feet away ignited a fierce determination within them. They couldn't afford to wait, to be passive victims in this dangerous game.

Waleed's mind raced as he desperately searched for a way out of the impending doom that seemed to hang over them.

He knew that they needed something – something big – to turn the tables and buy them a chance at survival. An idea sparked in Waleed's mind, a glimmer of hope amidst the darkness. It was a risky move, but he knew they had no other option left. Gathering every ounce of courage he had, he took a deep breath and shouted, 'Inspector Abdul Rashid! Wait! We need to tell you something important!'

The storage room seemed to vibrate with tension as the seconds ticked by. The boys exchanged anxious glances, their hearts pounding in their chests, unsure of whether Waleed's gamble would pay off. To their shock, the door to the storage room swung open, and in walked Inspector Abdul Rashid himself, followed closely by Rafiq. The dim light revealed their stern faces, their expressions a blend of curiosity and annoyance.

'What is it now?' Abdul Rashid's voice was laced with impatience, a dangerous glint in his eyes.

Waleed's heart raced, but he held his ground, his voice quivering only slightly as he spoke. 'Inspector, we have something you might want to know. Something that could change everything.'

Abdul Rashid's brows furrowed, a mix of skepticism and interest evident on his face. 'Speak quickly, then.'

Waleed took a deep breath and let the words tumble out. 'We have video evidence. Video evidence that implicates you. We have a recording of Tahir, the son of the minister, saying that you're the one managing the major drug network in Kashmir. He talks about your involvement, your control over everything.'

A tense silence settled in the room as Waleed's words hung in the air. The boys watched Abdul Rashid closely, studying his reactions for any sign of vulnerability. Rafiq's eyes darted between the boys and the inspector, a mix of surprise and worry clouding his expression.

Abdul Rashid's face hardened, his eyes narrowing as he considered the implications of Waleed's claim. 'And what do you intend to do with this supposed evidence?'

Waleed's voice held a flicker of confidence as he responded. 'We have a friend – a friend who's not here right now – who has this video. He's going to publish it online if anything happens to us. If we don't return safely, that video becomes public knowledge.'

A tense standoff ensued as the words hung in the air, the room heavy with the weight of the boys' threat. The boys held their breath, their hearts pounding, hoping that this unexpected turn of events would give them the upper hand.

In that charged moment, the power dynamic seemed to shift. The boys had played their hand, revealing a card that had the potential to bring down the very man who had sought to eliminate them. As they held their ground, they braced themselves for Abdul Rashid's response, ready to seize any opportunity that arose from this dangerous gamble.

Inspector Abdul Rashid's eyes bore into Waleed, his gaze a mix of calculation and frustration. 'You think I'll believe your claims based on some imaginary video? Do you really think I'm that gullible?'

Waleed's heart raced, but he refused to back down. He met the inspector's gaze head-on, his voice steady as he retorted, 'Call it imaginary if you want, but we know the truth. And the fact that you're even bothering to engage with us shows that you're not as confident as you're trying to appear.'

Abdul Rashid's lips curved into a chilling smile, his fingers' drumming on the table in a slow, deliberate rhythm. 'You're playing a dangerous game, boy. Do you really think your threats can save you?'

Waleed's voice grew firmer as he held his ground. 'We're not threatening you, Inspector. We're giving you a choice. Let us go, and we won't release the video. We won't expose you. It's your chance to escape this mess with your reputation intact.'

A tense silence descended upon the room as Abdul Rashid's eyes locked onto Waleed's. The air seemed to crackle with intensity, the stakes higher than ever before.

The inspector's expression shifted from amusement to something darker, a glint of anger lurking beneath the surface. 'You don't understand, do you? There's already a warrant out for my arrest. The police are after me. I don't care about my reputation anymore.'

Shahid chimed in, with his thoughts scrambling for a way to turn the situation in their favor. He leaned forward slightly, his voice taking on a calculated edge. 'You might not care about your reputation with the police, but what about the public? The evidence they have against you might be weak, but this video can change everything. You might escape the legal consequences, but you won't escape the court of public opinion.'

Abdul Rashid's expression faltered for a fraction of a second, a flicker of doubt crossing his face. The boys seized onto that moment, their hope kindling like a small flame in the darkness.

'We're giving you a chance to salvage whatever remains of your reputation,' Abrar pressed on. 'If you let us go, we won't release the video. It's your decision, Inspector.'

The room seemed to hold its breath as Abdul Rashid and the boys locked horns in a battle of wills. The tension was palpable, the outcome uncertain.

As the boys stood on the threshold of the storage room, hope slowly giving way to anxiety, Abdul Rashid's mocking laughter cut through the tense silence. It was a chilling sound, laced with arrogance and a dark sense of power. 'You think you're so clever, don't you? Believing you can outwit me and escape unscathed.'

Shahid's fists clenched, his jaw tight with determination. 'If you kill us, whole world is going to see the video.'

The inspector's eyes gleamed with a twisted amusement. He stepped closer to the boys, his voice dripping with condescension. 'Do you want to know how your dear friend Burhan? How he really died, do you? Let me enlighten you.'

He leaned in, his breath close to their ears, his voice dropping to a sinister whisper. 'Your friend was stupid, he had stopped buying drugs from my men. I don't mind that, I am losing a customer but it was fine, he was so stupid, he could have kept that to himself, why did he had to tell that to one of my guys,' he sneered, 'if anyone tries to leave and if they are rich we try to squeeze some extra money and my men asked him to pay 250,000 which he owed, and he agreed, they all agree.' He laughed. 'Although the next day he came with an empty bag saying he lost the money.' He walked to the door and smiled.

'Unluckily for him I was there that day, I was there in the house.' He paused and with an evil grin he continued, 'I just wanted to scare him, didn't plan to kill him, but I had a huge fight with wife on the phone, so my anger got the best of me.'

Abdul Rashid's laughter echoed off the walls, sending a shiver down their spines. 'He couldn't handle a simple beating, and he crumbled like a house of cards, the irony is that even though I have killed many strong and connected men, but never could have imagined that weasel will cause this much trouble for me.'

Rafiq was standing by the door, and he knew Abdul Rashid was lying and it was more than a simple beating, He could still remember that scene like it was yesterday, Burhan came to meet Ather at the drug house and at the corridor Burhan was pleading for a few more days till he can make the payment and inspector Rashid was listening in from the corridor. Rashid ran towards Burhan and started beating him. Ather tried to stop Rashid but looking at blood in his eyes he was too afraid to step up. He just kept watching in horror as Abdul Rashid kept hitting him. He had beaten Burhan so severely that he succumbed to the injuries, even when Burhan had collapsed and was barely moving Abdul Rashid kept hitting him in a fit of Anger After a while Abdul Rashid sat down next to Burhan and then he noticed he had stopped breathing, he ordered Ather and Rafiq to check if he was alive. Ather was shocked as this was the first time, he had witnessed someone killed in front of him, he just couldn't speak, and Abdul Rashid disgustingly looked at Ather and told him to clean up and go home. Abdul Rashid then ordered Rafiq to make sure to death of Burhan look like a stabbing which were becoming popular in the region and throw his body somewhere near the city.

The boys were heartbroken as they could visualize what Burhan had gone through. Shahid's anger flared, his fists trembling with a mixture of rage and grief. 'You murdered him in cold blood!'

The inspector's eyes bore into Shahid's, a twisted smile playing on his lips. 'Oh, he was weak, just like you boys. He never understood how close he was to wolf's den and started playing with the wolf's food.'

Abdul Rashid's laughter had a haunting quality to it as he shared his bitter sentiments. 'It's not just you boys all Kashmiri people, insects, that's what they are. Protesting India and marching for freedom yet clutching their Indian passports like it means something. You all should just vanish, you know why I trust Rafiq, because he is from Jammu, not like you fucking disloyal dogs.'

Abrar's fists clenched involuntarily, his face contorting with a mix of anger and indignation. 'How can you say that? How can you hate your own people so much?'

Abdul Rashid's eyes gleamed with a twisted amusement, as if savoring the discomfort, he had caused. 'Hate? Hate is a weak word, my boy. I despise them. They think they're entitled to their voices, their rights. But in the grand scheme of things, they're nothing.'

Waleed's voice shook with a mixture of disbelief and disgust. 'You're a part of them too, Abdul Rashid. You were born here.'

A sneer formed on Abdul Rashid's lips. 'Watch it, don't you dare call me Kashmiri. You are all pests, annoying and insignificant.'

Abrar's eyes blazed with intensity. 'We didn't choose this occupation. We didn't ask for the turmoil that surrounds us.

And we certainly didn't ask for your drugs poisoning our streets.'

The tension in the room grew palpable, the air heavy with the weight of their confrontation. Abdul Rashid's gaze bore into Abrar's, a twisted mix of amusement and malice. 'You're a feisty one, aren't you? But mark my words, your defiance won't save you.'

Abrar's voice was laced with fury. 'You're a monster.'

Abdul Rashid's gaze shifted from one boy to another, a predator sizing up its prey. 'Am I? Or am I just a man who's seen the reality of this world? A world where power rules and the weak are discarded like trash.'

He turned away, his laughter fading into the distance. 'You're lucky you're still alive, for now. But don't think for a second that you can escape me. I'll be watching you guys.'

With those ominous words hanging in the air, the inspector left the room, leaving the boys in a state of shock and disbelief. They were left to grapple with the horrifying truth about Burhan's death and the darkness that lurked within the man who was supposed to protect and serve.

# Chapter 15
# Save the Soul

Insha strode down the dingy corridor of the CID headquarters, the tap of her boots echoing off the peeling walls. Reaching the IT department, she threw open the door without knocking.

Inside, a dozen officers lazed around, feet up on cluttered desks. The air was hazy with cigarette smoke and the smell of stale sweat. Insha crinkled her nose in disgust as all eyes turned to her.

'Where is Officer Maqbool from IT cell!' She bellowed.

'We may have a hostage situation and I need your team tracing a phone now!'

The IT head, a portly man with yellowing teeth, smirked. 'Well, well…if it isn't our little spitfire Inspector Insha. To what do we owe this pleasure?' His beady eyes raked over Insha luridly.

Insha slammed her fist on his desk. 'Cut the crap, Maqbool. Three innocent lives hang in the balance while you waste time making lewd jokes. I'm not asking again – get your team on this, NOW!'

Maqbool leaned back, unaffected by her outburst. 'Keep your burqa on, sweetheart. We don't take orders from you.'

The other men laughed, their cigarette-stained lips curled in sneers.

'It's your buddy Abdul Rashid,' Insha spat out. 'While you prop your fat legs up, that monster roams free with children hostage. Does that mean nothing to you?'

A tense silence followed. Then Maqbool grinned, his paan-stained teeth on display.

'Rules are rules. No surveillance access without the Commissioner's orders.' He picked his ear nonchalantly, watching Insha's face flush with anger.

'Those children will die! Have you no basic humanity?' Insha pleaded desperately. But she knew these corrupt souls were devoid of conscience.

Maqbool blew her a mocking kiss. 'Now run along Insha darling, before you miss your kitty party. Let the real men handle police work.'

His raucous laughter followed Insha as she stormed out, blood boiling. She had hit another dead end. Once again, corruption had won out over moral duty. But she wasn't licked yet.

Insha Khan's fingers flew over the keys of her phone as she dialed the number of the police commissioner. The urgency of the situation weighed heavily on her, and she needed his swift approval to initiate the tracking process.

The phone rang a few times before the commissioner's voice came through, authoritative and composed. 'Commissioner Ashwin speaking.'

'Sir, it's Insha Khan,' she responded, her voice carrying a sense of urgency. 'I need your immediate approval to track the location of Abdul Rashid and one of his men through their phones.'

There was a brief pause on the other end of the line, as if the commissioner was considering the gravity of her request. 'Were you not able to catch him?'

Insha's tone remained resolute. 'No, sir, he had fled already, he has many friends in the force that are helping him. I have reason to believe that he is holding three individuals against their will. I need to ensure their safety and bring him to justice.'

The commissioner's voice remained stern as he replied, 'I understand the situation, Insha. I'll grant you the approval, but make sure you follow proper protocol.'

'Thank you, sir,' Insha said with gratitude in her voice. 'I'll ensure that everything is done by the book.'

With the commissioner's approval secured, Insha burst back into the CID office, she declared, 'The Commissioner has authorized full surveillance access. Get your team on it immediately!'

Seeing Insha's iron-willed expression, Maqbool didn't dare object this time. Sullenly he barked orders at his team. Insha added, 'No one leaves this room until Rashid is found. I want all mobile phones surrendered – we have a mole, and I won't let them tip off Rashid again.'

Grudgingly, the officers complied, realizing Insha meant business. She stationed officers at the door to enforce the lockdown.

'We have just one chance to catch this guy,' she addressed the room.

'Fail me again and you will face dire consequences.' As the digital pathways were established to trace the locations of Abdul Rashid and Rafiq's phones, Insha felt a surge of determination. She was on the cusp of a breakthrough, and she was resolute in her mission to rescue the boys and bring down the corruption that had woven its dark web around them.

Abdul Rashid was smart, and his last location was pinged at his home, but Rafiq's location was showing at the old brick factory at the other end of the city. After checking in with the informant, Insha was certain that this is likely location, Abdul Rashid is hiding and holding the boys at. Insha Khan, called a few officers whom she still trusted and asked them to join her for a mission but being careful she didn't share many details.

As Insha Khan prepared for the upcoming raid on the cement factory, she knew that this operation was both crucial and dangerous. Following protocol and taking into consideration the sensitivity of the mission, she decided to inform the Indian army that they were going for an ambush and might need their assistance.

Her team members, however, questioned the decision to involve the army. They gathered around her, their expressions a mix of concern and doubt. One of them spoke up, 'Insha, I understand this is a critical operation, but isn't calling in the army a bit too risky? This is a sensitive area, and they are known for just shooting everything in their path.'

Insha Khan paused, weighing the pros and cons of her decision. She understood the gravity of the situation and the potential consequences of involving the army. However, she also knew the risks they faced without additional support.

She replied, 'I hear your concerns, and I share them. But we can't underestimate the opposition we might encounter. We're dealing with a well-organized network here. I don't know how many men has there right now, it could be 5 or it could be 50. Calling in the army might be our best option to ensure we have the necessary firepower and resources.'

The team members exchanged uneasy glances, realizing the weight of the decision. Insha Khan continued, 'We'll proceed with caution and coordination. Our primary objective is to apprehend those responsible and minimize any civilian disruptions. I'll keep communication open with the army and request their support only if the situation demands it. Our goal is to bring these criminals to justice while maintaining the peace. We're in this together, and we'll make the right call when the time comes.'

With that, the team readied themselves for the impending operation, aware of the delicate balance they needed to maintain between taking down the criminal network and preserving the peace in this sensitive region.

'Listen up,' Insha addressed her team, her voice firm and commanding. 'Our mission and top priority is to apprehend Abdul Rashid and Rafiq. We don't know what we're walking into, so stay alert and follow my lead. We're going in fast and coordinated and if we find those boys, don't shoot!'

The officers nodded in agreement, their expressions focused and resolute. They were a team forged by trust and a shared commitment to upholding justice. Insha could see the determination in their eyes, and it strengthened her resolve.

With the briefing concluded, they moved swiftly to their vehicles, the tension in the air palpable. Insha's heart raced as they began the drive towards the location provided by the IT cell. The streets of the city passed by in a blur as they closed in on their destination.

As they approached the location, the tension inside the vehicle grew even more intense. Insha's grip on car seat tightened, her mind racing through possible scenarios. The officers exchanged determined glances, each one aware of the risks but ready to face them head-on.

Finally, they arrived at the location, a nondescript building tucked away in a quiet corner. Insha's heart pounded in her chest as she signaled to her team to surround the area. They moved with calculated precision, each officer taking their position, ready to breach the building and confront the criminals within.

The factory was in a rundown industrial area on the outskirts of the city. It was an old brick building with faded and peeling paint, hinting at years of neglect. The exterior walls were stained black in some areas from decades of exhaust fumes billowing from the chimney stacks. Rows of grimy windows lined the sides, most of them cracked or missing panes. A high barbed wire fence surrounded the premises and beyond the fence, the grounds were unkempt, with weeds poking through cracks in the pitted concrete.

The storage areas located in the back had a dilapidated feel, with old wooden crates piled high. The rooms were dimly lit, with exposed pipes and flickering lights overhead. It was in these neglected rooms that illicit activities took place, far from prying eyes. Overall, the factory exterior projected an aura of abandonment, but it was the activities concealed within its walls that revealed its secrets. It was a façade that hid a dangerous underworld in plain sight.

Insha's radio crackled to life as she received confirmation that the perimeter was secure. Taking a deep breath, she nodded to the officers around her. It was time to move. With weapons drawn, they approached the building, the tension building with each step. Insha's mind was focused, her training kicking in as she prepared to lead the operation. As they breached the door, the adrenaline surged through her veins.

As per the protocol, they cordoned the area and using a portable loudspeaker Insha Khan announced, 'Abdul Rashid, come out with your hands in the air and ask your men to come out as well with hands in the air.' Insha's voice rang out, commanding and unwavering.

Abdul Rashid was caught by surprise as he was sitting on old rusty sofa drinking his whisky, he sprung up and peeped outside the windows and whispered to his team, 'Get ready and get armed,' while laying low.

Insha Khan kept repeating the message through the loud speaker this time adding, 'We have this whole area surrounded and you won't get far easily, let's do this non-violently.'

Abdul Rashid while laying low, I am very sure she has maximum if 5–6 people with her and we can easily take them. There was a moment of hesitation, and then Abdul Rashid's expression twisted into a mixture of anger and frustration. He picked up his pistol, shouting from the window, 'If you want us, come and get us.'

As Insha Khan's team engaged in a tense standoff with Abdul Rashid's group, the boys seized the opportunity to take action. Their hearts pounded in their chests as they realized that their only chance of escape lay in breaking the lock on the storage room door. From the crack of the door, they could see that door was closed by a latch lock which could be opened if they could fit something through the crack and push the latch open.

Abrar knelt beside the stubborn lock, his trembling fingers fumbling with a makeshift tool he'd cobbled together from a stray piece of metal. Beside him, Shahid and Waleed watched with bated breath, their eyes fixed on his desperate attempts. The cacophony of the ongoing confrontation outside both masked their efforts and added to their sense of urgency.

The lock, however, refused to yield. Abrar's hands shook with a volatile mix of fear and adrenaline, but failure was not an option. Their lives hung precariously in the balance. As Insha's commanding voice echoed through the air, demanding Abdul Rashid's surrender, the tension inside the room reached a fever pitch. Her orders were punctuated by warning shots fired into the air by her men, intended to coerce Abdul Rashid and his accomplices into submission. For the boys, the world outside was a chaotic symphony of peril.

Abrar's fingers moved with frantic determination, each second passing like an eternity. The lock seemed impervious to his efforts, and it held their escape hostage. Sensing the urgency, Shahid took a step back and began delivering powerful kicks to the door. With each resounding thud, the lock seemed to relent, the door gradually yielding to their relentless assault.

One of Rafiq's henchmen had been alerted by the loud noise from the storage room. He approached cautiously and saw the lock of the storage room had been broken. The boys, who had concealed themselves behind crates and boxes, burst into action. Shahid, in a split-second decision, wielded a broken shovel as his makeshift weapon and hit the henchman on the head.

With the immediate threat neutralized, they made their way toward the main gate, their hearts pounding in their chests. However, they were abruptly halted in their tracks as chaos erupted around them. Police forces and Abdul Rashid's men engaged in a fierce firefight, and the boys found themselves trapped in a deadly crossfire. In the darkness, bullets whizzed past, and the boys realized they had become unwitting participants in a harrowing battle for survival.

Amidst the deafening exchange of gunfire, the boys navigated their way through the perilous battleground like phantoms in the night. The air was thick with the acrid scent of gunpowder, and the incessant cracks of gunfire echoed all around them. Each step they took was fraught with danger, but they were driven by an unrelenting determination to escape this nightmarish ordeal.

Bullets whizzed perilously close, the stinging sensation of narrowly avoided disaster a constant companion. Shahid's instincts guided them through the labyrinthine network of crates and storage units, his quick thinking helping them evade death multiple times. Abrar and Waleed clung to Shahid's every move, their trust in their friend unwavering. As they darted between cover and concealment, they couldn't help but reflect on the many challenges they had faced together over the years. From their innocent childhood games to the complexities of their friendship forged in adversity, their bond had always seen them through.

Amid the chaos, they saw several of Abdul Rashid's men fall to the ground, their bodies motionless. Suddenly they saw a towering figure run towards the main door, he was able to suppress their fire and was even able to take down a few police personnel, although as he tried to reload his rifle, his eyes shifted to the boys who are hiding behind the bags of cement. He looked at them and realized that they were to blame for all of this, in a fraction of a second his amazement turned to rage, and he pointed his rifle towards the boys and was ready to shoot. A terrible resolve etched across his features, his finger tightened on the trigger, ready to unleash a hail of deadly bullets. Yet, fate, ever fickle, intervened, a stray bullet, fired by one of his own men in the heat of the melee, found its mark with eerie precision. The projectile met the temple of the towering figure, and in an instant, he crumpled like a marionette with severed strings, his colossal frame tumbling to the ground in lifeless surrender.

For Abrar, Shahid, and Waleed, this night would forever be etched in their memories as a night of survival, a night when they had come face to face with the darkest aspects of human nature. As the gunfire gradually subsided, the boys cautiously made their way towards the exit. They navigated through the aftermath of the fierce confrontation. As they were about to cross the main gate, Abdul Rashid, his face contorted with pain from the flesh wound in his leg, stumbled upon the boys as they cautiously made their way through the chaotic aftermath of the gunfight. His eyes locked onto them, and in his desperation, he saw an opportunity for escape. He approached them with a malevolent grin, using his wounded leg as leverage.

'Boys.' He hissed through gritted teeth. 'Get over here. You're coming with me.' His voice was laced with a chilling threat.

Abrar, Shahid, and Waleed froze, their hearts sinking as they realized the danger they were now in. Abdul Rashid's reputation as a ruthless criminal was well-known, he was armed with a gun, and they had no doubt that he would stop at nothing to evade capture.

Reluctantly, they obeyed his command, moving closer to him. With a painful limp, Abdul Rashid guided them to a nearby vehicle, his grip on their arms unyielding. The boys were now his shield, and he had no qualms about using them to make his getaway. He sat in the back asked one of them to drive which pointing his gun on all three. Abdul Rashid painfully took out the key from his jacket and threw at Shahid. Shahid nervously turned the key, the car's engine roared to life, and they sped away from the scene of the intense firefight, leaving behind a trail of chaos and destruction. Insha Khan and the other police officers had been close and were seconds late in catching Abdul Rashid.

Insha Khan's urgent pursuit took her to the police van, her shouts cutting through the tension: 'Don't shoot, don't shoot!' Her heart raced as she got closer to the fleeing suspects. Just as she began the chase, her phone rang. It was the army commander, his voice laced with concern.

'Hello, Ms. Khan,' he said. 'Are you OK? We could hear the gunshots all the way here in the city.'

Insha Khan, knowing she had to maintain her composure despite the intense situation, replied, 'Thank you for calling, but I am in the middle of a chase. I'll have to call you back, sir.'

The urgency in the commander's voice was evident as he responded, 'Before you disconnect, we've deployed a small convoy to assist you. They'll be there soon, just in case you need help.'

Insha Khan hesitated for a moment; her apprehension hidden beneath a veneer of diplomacy. 'Thank you, but everything is under control for now. We've already taken down at least a dozen men involved in the drug trade.'

The commander pressed further, 'Let us help, madam. We want to be a part of your success. It's essential for us to show that we're contributing positively to this society.'

Insha Khan, torn between accepting assistance and maintaining her independence, chose to disconnect the call without giving a definitive response. She knew that every decision she made in the heat of the chase could have far-reaching consequences, and she was determined to bring the criminals to justice while preserving the integrity of her operation.

Inside the car, the boys exchanged fearful glances, their hearts heavy with dread. They knew that their ordeal was far from over, and the road ahead was fraught with uncertainty. The sound of sirens wailed in the distance, growing closer with each passing moment. Insha, her eyes fixed on the speeding car carrying Abdul Rashid and the boys, gritted her teeth and accelerated. Her heart pounded with a mix of anxiety and determination.

The chase through the darkened streets of Srinagar was intense. Abdul Rashid, his wounded leg throbbing with pain, pushed the car to its limits. He shouted at Shahid who was driving the car, 'If they catch us, I will shoot all of you and then I will shoot myself.' Shahid swerved through narrow alleyways, hoping to lose his pursuers, but Insha Khan was relentless. The boys, trapped in the car, could feel the tension escalating. They exchanged anxious glances, silently praying for a way out of this perilous situation. The cacophony of police sirens and the screeching tires filled the air as the chase raged on.

Insha's radio crackled with updates from her team, her grip on the steering wheel tightened as she wove through the labyrinthine streets, her mind focused solely on the mission at hand. But Abdul Rashid while in pain looked outside and realized, he knew this area, so he shouted at Shahid, take a left and as the police cars followed, he then demanded Shahid to go off-road as soon as the next turn comes up as it leads into a field, the police cars won't be able to catch up. Shahid knew he had no choice but to agree and as soon as he saw the next turn, he took the off-road which led them to a field a few meters lower than the road and after a few meters stopped the car. Moments later, the police cars passed through the road, unknown of the trick played by Abdul Rashid.

Abdul Rashid waited for a while and then shouted at the boys to get out. As the boys exited the car, he grunted in pain while trying to exit the car himself. As Abdul Rashid stumbled out of the car, the dim glow of the moon revealed the extent of his injuries. His leg wound had bled profusely during the chaotic escape, and he could feel his strength waning rapidly. His vision blurred, and he struggled to maintain consciousness. Around him lay an open field, the silvery light illuminating rows of crops swaying gently in the night breeze. In the distance, dark silhouettes of trees stood like silent sentinels watching this unfolding drama.

His wounded leg throbbed with each agonizing step as he hobbled away from the car. The weight of his actions bore down on him, crushing his spirit. Just hours ago, he had been filled with fiery determination to evade capture at any cost. But now, in this moon glow-bathed clearing, with only the three boys and the looming trees as his audience, his blazing anger began to melt away.

Exhaustion and remorse flooded through Abdul Rashid's body in waves. He thought of the violence he had unleashed, the lives endangered. His wife's face flashed in his mind, her sad eyes the last time he saw her, his young son clinging to her hand. What had he become? The man who had once lived a simple life, who cherished his family over everything else, seemed a stranger to him now.

Disgusted at the desperation that had corroded his soul, Abdul Rashid raised his eyes to the infinite sky above. The stars gazed back silently as though reflecting the lost shards of his humanity. Here in this isolated field, far from the city that had led him astray, he was finally forced to confront the nightmare his choices had created.

The boys were afraid and bruised, their bodies and minds battered by the night's traumatic events. This was nothing like the action movies they had seen, where heroes dodged bullets and confronted villains effortlessly. In real life, having a loaded gun pointed at you was utterly terrifying in a way they had never imagined. When Abdul Rashid had pressed that cold, hard metal against them, they instinctively sensed the deadly power contained in the weapon. They could almost feel the weight of the bullets, picture the damage one could inflict if fired at close range. A gun in real life was not a prop or special effect – it was an instrument of death, and they were at the mercy of the man wielding it.

Abdul Rashid sat on the ground leaning on the car tire and began to speak. His voice trembled with a mixture of exhaustion, agony, and profound remorse.

'Listen to me,' he implored, his eyes filled with a haunting sadness. 'I was once a different man, a man with dreams, a family, and a future. I never wanted any of this.'

His words hung heavy in the air, and the boys couldn't help but listen, captivated by the unexpected vulnerability in their captor's voice.

Abdul Rashid continued, 'I have a wife and a son, we lived a simple life. I worked an honest job, struggling to make ends meet. But desperation, they change a man.'

Tears welled in his eyes as he recalled the choices that had led him down this dark path. 'I didn't get involved in the drug trade, thinking it would provide a better life for my family, but I thought I could control it, although it controlled me. It consumed me.'

The boys watched, their fear slowly giving way to a strange empathy, as Abdul Rashid's voice cracked with the weight of his confession. 'My wife left me, taking my son with her. She couldn't bear to watch what I had become. And now, look at me, a criminal, a fugitive.'

He sank to his knees, his face buried in his hands, and the forest seemed to echo with the weight of his regret. 'How quickly I regret every choice I made, every life. I ruined, every family torn apart by my actions. I would give anything to turn back time, to be the man I once was.' With those words he dropped the gun on his lap.

In that surreal moment, the forest bore witness to the raw and painful confession of a man who had lost everything. The boys, now deeply moved by the depths of his remorse, faced a decision of their own – whether to help the man who had held them captive or to let him face the consequences of his actions.

Abdul Rashid's fate hung in the balance, and the forest remained cloaked in an unsettling silence, awaiting their choice. Their empathy overpowered their anger, and they knew they couldn't let a wounded man die alone in the forest. Waleed, with his simple and compassionate heart, took the lead. He gently approached Abdul Rashid, who was now sitting on the ground, weakened and disoriented.

Burhan and Shahid, though still wary, offered their support to help Abdul Rashid. They found a piece of cloth to temporarily dress his wound, stemming the bleeding as best they could. Abdul Rashid, in his weak and blurred state, managed a faint, almost ironic smile.

'You're right,' Waleed whispered, his voice filled with unexpected sympathy. 'You killed our friend, who was nothing short of an angel, he fought addiction, studied hard for his exams and all of that was wasted because of you.' Waleed paused trying to hold his emotions. 'Still we "Kashmiri" men are helping you with your wounds now, what does that tell you.'

'Thank you,' he murmured, his voice barely audible. 'I am sorry for…everything.' before collapsing to his side.

As they sat together in that quiet forest, Abdul Rashid's words lingered in the air, a somber reminder that even in the darkest of circumstances, humanity could find a glimmer of redemption. A few moments later, a tense hush falls over the desolate field. Waleed, filled with a strange mix of fear and desperation, tries to move the gun that had once been in Abdul Rashid's lap.

Suddenly, the silence is shattered as two massive army trucks, their bright headlights cutting through the darkness like blades, screech to a halt on the road. Waleed, caught off guard, reacted with sheer panic, without thinking, he tosses the gun to the side, the metallic clatter creating a distinctive sound of a weapon.

There is a silence in that air, except of the sound of engines resting, suddenly a few men jump out of the trucks and shouted some codes which could just be gibberish to the boys. They moved closer, shouting even louder and suddenly there are shots fired at the boys. Terrified, the boys stumble backward, seeking cover behind the nearest available refuge, which happens to be the car. In their desperation, they cry out, their voices trembling with fear, 'We're not with them! We're innocent!'

Amid this chaotic and nerve-wracking moment, Insha Khan's police van screeches to a halt beside the massive army trucks. She emerges with authority, her voice cutting through the mayhem as she urgently orders the armed soldiers to cease their fire.

Shahid and Abrar were overwhelmed with relief when they heard Insha Khan ordering the army men to stop shooting. It felt like a glimmer of hope in their darkest moment. However, their joy was short-lived as they noticed Waleed, who had fallen to the ground, clutching his abdomen. A deep, crimson stain was rapidly spreading across his clothes, and it was evident that he was bleeding profusely. Panic set in as they rushed to Waleed's side, their hearts pounding with fear for their friend.

'Help! Help, our friend's been shot,' Shahid cried out desperately. Insha Khan and her team swiftly moved to assess the situation and provide first aid, realizing that this was now a matter of life and death.

As Insha Khan swiftly called for an ambulance on her radio, the atmosphere remained tense and fraught with anxiety. The boys, huddled around their wounded friend, were unable to contain their fear and sorrow. Tears streamed down their faces, their voices a poignant contrast to the violence that had unfolded throughout this treacherous night.

Their cries pierced the darkness, carrying the weight of the horrors they had endured. Insha Khan's radio message hung in the air, a lifeline in the midst of chaos, as the wounded Waleed fought to hold on, and his friends clung to the hope that help would arrive in time to save their dear companion.

Insha Khan's fury simmered as she confronted the army men, her voice laced with anger and disbelief. She demanded, 'Why did you open fire on these boys? They were unarmed and posed no threat.'

One of the army men, defensive and unwilling to back down, retorted, 'Madam, we are just doing our job. We didn't have the luxury to ask questions. We spotted a pistol near them, and it seemed like these were the individuals you were in pursuit of.'

Insha Khan, her eyes heavy with exhaustion and worry, responded firmly, 'They are just young boys. This isn't how we conduct an operation. Is this how you ensure the safety of innocent civilians.'

The army man glared at Insha Khan with a hint of disgust and frustration before he turned away, refusing to engage further. The tension in the air was palpable as Insha Khan focused on tending to the injured boys, anger and disappointment etched into her expression.

As Insha Khan and her team worked frantically to control Waleed's bleeding, the other officers turned their attention to keeping the injured boy awake. They gathered around Waleed, their faces marked with concern, and offered words of reassurance and support.

'Stay with us, son,' one of the officers said, his voice quivering with empathy. 'You're going to be just fine. We're here with you.'

Abrar and Shahid, their own eyes moist with tears, joined in the encouragement. 'You're strong, Waleed. We have to go Patan and eat the apples of your orchid,' Shahid whispered, his voice choked with emotion. 'We can't lose you, Walleed, please stay with us.'

Abrar added with a trembling smile, 'You're going to pull through this, buddy. We still have a lot of adventures ahead of us.'

As the ambulance arrived, the team swiftly moved Waleed onto the stretcher and into the vehicle. Panic was in the air as they realized that Waleed had lost his pulse. Without wasting a second, they began CPR, working frantically to revive their dear friend.

Abrar and Shahid stood nearby; their eyes locked on the heartbreaking scene unfolding before them. They watched with bated breath, their hearts heavy with dread, as the paramedics fought to bring life back into their friend's fragile body. Every chest compression and breath were a desperate plea for Waleed to return to them, to be the most forgiving and cheerful friend they had always known.

The ambulance's siren wailed through the night as it sped towards the nearest hospital, with Abrar and Shahid by their injured friend's side, praying for a miracle.

As the ambulance screeched to a halt at the hospital's entrance, a desolate stillness enveloped the night. Abrar and Shahid, their tears flowing uncontrollably, staggered out of the vehicle, their hearts shattered into countless pieces. They watched as the paramedics solemnly and gently moved

Waleed's lifeless body from the ambulance, the cruel reality of his passing sinking in like an anchor pulling them into the depths of despair.

Time itself seemed to slow down for Abrar and Shahid, the world around them fading into an indistinct blur. The weight of injustice and the unbearable loss pressed down upon their chests, leaving them gasping for breath. They wanted to scream, to vent their anguish and anger at a world that could be so ruthless and unforgiving.

The hospital's sterile walls echoed with their sorrow, a poignant reminder of the profound injustice that had torn their friend away from them. In that agonizing moment, as they stood by Waleed's side, they clung to each other, their bond as friends and survivors stronger than ever, even in the face of this unrelenting cruelty.

Insha Khan, who had been closely trailing the ambulance in her police van, rushed to the side of the grieving boys as they stood there, overwhelmed by sorrow and disbelief. Her heart ached for them, and she knew that no words could fill the void that the death of their friend had just created.

After a few hours of numbing grief and shared tears, Shahid's parents and Abrar's mother rushed to the hospital. Their faces etched with worry and anxiety, they yearned to embrace their sons, to hold them close, and offer what little comfort they could during this unthinkable ordeal.

Shahid and Abrar, their eyes swollen from crying and their hearts heavy with sorrow, saw their parents' faces as they entered the hospital room. In that poignant moment, it was as if the weight of their loss was shared by all who loved them. There were no words that could express the depth of the pain they felt, but the embrace of family offered a flicker of solace in the darkness of despair.

After the initial shock and grief had settled to some extent, Shahid and Abrar began to notice the pain they had unknowingly suppressed amidst the chaos of the night. The beatings they had endured at the hands of Abdul Rashid's men had left them with injuries that they hadn't even registered in the midst of their frantic escape.

Abrar, wincing as he shifted in his hospital bed, touched the tender, swollen area on his side where he had been kicked repeatedly. The sharp stinging pain was a stark reminder of the brutality they had faced. Shahid, lying in the adjacent bed, gingerly touched his face, which still bore traces of the blows he had received.

It was their family members who persuaded them to seek medical attention. After the initial rush of emotions following Waleed's death, Shahid's parents and Abrar's mother turned their attention to their sons' well-being. They insisted that they should receive a thorough medical examination. Doctors, recognizing the signs of physical trauma, agreed that it was necessary.

The hospital staff conducted a series of tests and examinations, confirming that Shahid and Abrar had indeed sustained injuries during their ordeal. Both young men were admitted to the hospital for further care and observation. Despite their pain and exhaustion, Shahid and Abrar found a semblance of comfort in the presence of their families, who remained steadfast by their sides during this difficult period.

In the days that followed, they would not only grieve Waleed but also recover from their own physical and emotional wounds. As they lay in their hospital beds, they replayed the treacherous night that had occurred and how they lost yet another friend.

As the days passed, Insha Khan continued to extend her support to the boys. She recognized the immense danger they had faced and the trauma they had endured. She arranged for counselling to help them process their experiences and cope with the emotional aftermath. Gradually, a sense of trust began to develop between the boys and Insha Khan. They understood that, in her own way, she had been looking out for them and had been fighting her own battles.

After several days of medical care and counselling, Insha Khan visited them one evening in the hospital, bearing both good and bad news. She explained that, for the sake of public perception and the reputation of the police department, the official story would be that Abdul Rashid had tragically lost his life while chasing the drug smugglers. It was a bitter pill to swallow for the boys, who knew the truth of the matter all too well. Abdul Rashid was the mastermind behind the major Drug network and responsible for many deaths including Burhan's.

Insha Khan, seeing their disappointment, offered some words of solace. 'I understand this is difficult to accept,' she said, her voice filled with empathy. 'But the police force is never going to admit that one of their own had been running a drug empire behind their back and this will implicate many powerful people. Sometimes, we have to make difficult choices. Insha paused and the continued. Plus, the good news is that you can go home now.'

The boys nodded, reluctantly acknowledging the necessity of such a decision. They had come to understand that justice, in the real world, was not always straightforward.

It required compromises, secrets, and the navigation of moral gray areas. But deep down, they held onto the hope that their testimony, their experiences, would still contribute to dismantling the drug network that had wreaked havoc on their lives and their city. Insha Khan assured them that their safety would be a top priority, and they could always reach out to her if they needed assistance or protection. With a final nod of gratitude, the boys watched her leave, carrying with her the burden of their shared secrets.

As they closed the door behind her, they couldn't help but feel a sense of unease. The world outside was far more complex and treacherous than they had ever imagined, and the path to justice would be fraught with challenges and compromises. As they sat in the hospital bed, watching the news, they couldn't help but feel a sense of frustration and anger. The world at large would never know the full extent of the corrupt drug empire that Abdul Rashid had presided over, nor the horrors they had endured in its midst. It was a harsh reality check, a reminder of the murky waters of politics and power that often obscured the truth.

Several months had passed since the tragic events that had forever altered the course of their lives. On a quiet afternoon, Abrar and Shahid embarked on a solemn journey to visit the resting places of their dear friends, Burhan and Waleed. The cemetery they sought was a serene sanctuary, embraced by the gentle warmth of the afternoon sun filtering through the trees.

Upon reaching the headstones bearing the names of Burhan and Waleed, they were greeted by a sight that tugged at their hearts. With reverence, Abrar knelt beside Burhan's resting place, his gentle hands carefully tending to the area.

Shahid, equally determined to honor his friends' memory, set about clearing the encroaching weeds that had encircled the graves.

Sitting beside these hallowed grounds, their emotions welled up within them. The recollection of times not too long ago, filled with laughter and joy, overwhelmed them. In those days, the bonds of friendship had been unbreakable, with Burhan and Waleed standing out as the most loving and generous of them all. Now, only Abrar and Shahid remained, and their loss was a heavy burden to bear.

Tears flowed freely as they allowed the memories of their lost friends to wash over them, like a gentle but persistent tide. Side by side, they offered their prayers. Their whispered Arabic supplications drifted into the air, each word a tribute to the friends they had lost. In that peaceful moment, it felt as though the spirits of Burhan and Waleed were present, as tangible as the earth beneath them.

Dabbing away their tears, Abrar and Shahid stood in silence. Without exchanging words, their actions spoke volumes. Shahid produced a phone stand and placed it carefully on Waleed's headstone, while Abrar positioned his phone upon it.

Together, they initiated a video recording, capturing this moment for a purpose that transcended grief.

Shahid's voice quivered slightly as he began, 'I am Shahid Iqbal.'

And then Abrar's steady voice joined in, 'I am Abrar Qazi.'

'We are making this video to tell you what really happened with the recent police drug scandal and the involvement of inspector Abdul Rashid, also about the death of Burhan and Walled from Islamia College.'